NEW APPROACHES IN SOCIOLOGY
Studies in Social Inequality, Social Change, and Social Justice

Edited by
Nancy A. Naples
University of Connecticut

A ROUTLEDGE SERIES

New Approaches in Sociology
Studies in Social Inequality, Social Change, and Social Justice
Nancy A. Naples, *General Editor*

The Social Organization of Policy
An Institutional Ethnography of UN Forest Deliberations
Lauren E. Eastwood

The Struggle over Gay, Lesbian, and Bisexual Rights
Facing Off in Cincinnati
Kimberly B. Dugan

Parenting for the State
An Ethnographic Analysis of Non-Profit Foster Care
Teresa Toguchi Swartz

Talking Back to Psychiatry
The Psychiatric Consumer/Survivor/Ex-Patient Movement
Linda J. Morrison

Contextualizing Homelessness
Critical Theory, Homelessness, and Federal Policy Addressing the Homeless
Ken Kyle

Linking Activism
Ecology, Social Justice, and Education for Social Change
Morgan Gardner

The Everyday Lives of Sex Workers in the Netherlands
Katherine Gregory

Striving and Surviving
A Daily Life Analysis of Honduran Transnational Families
Leah Schmalzbauer

STRIVING AND SURVIVING
A Daily Life Analysis of Honduran Transnational Families

Leah Schmalzbauer

LONDON AND NEW YORK

Published 2005 by Routledge
2 Park Square, Milton Park, Abingdon, Oxon OX14 4RN
52 Vanderbilt Avenue, New York, NY 10017

Routledge is an imprint of the Taylor & Francis Group, an informa business

© 2005 by Taylor & Francis Group, LLC

First issued in paperback 2013

International Standard Book Number-13: 978-0-415-65203-2 (Paperback)
Library of Congress Card Number 2005016654

All rights reserved. No part of this book may be reprinted or reproduced or utilised in any form or by any electronic, mechanical, or other means, now known or hereafter invented, including photocopying and recording, or in any information storage or retrieval system, without permission in writing from the publishers.

Notice:

Product or corporate names may be trademarks or registered trademarks, and are used only for identification and explanation without intent to infringe.

Library of Congress Cataloging-in-Publication Data

Schmalzbauer, Leah.
    Striving and surviving : a daily life analysis of Honduran transnational families / Leah Schmalzbauer.
       p. cm. -- (New approaches in sociology)
    Includes bibliographical references and index.
    ISBN 0-415-97593-X
    1. Honduras--Emigration and immigration. 2. Hondurans--United States--Economic conditions.
3. Emigrant remittances--Honduras. 4. Households--Honduras. I. Title. II. Series.

JV7419.S36 2005
306.3'086'9120973--dc22   2005016654

*For Mom and Dad
with love*

Contents

Acknowledgments ix

Introduction
Transnational Families and Daily Life 1

Chapter One
Surviving in the Margins, Struggling to Move Up 19

Chapter Two
Strategies and Challenges of Transnational Care 49

Chapter Three
A Week in the Life 75

Chapter Four
Transamerican Dreams 91

Conclusion
Para Seguir Adelante, To Continue Moving Forward 111

References 119

Index 127

Acknowledgments

I could not have successfully completed this project without the transnational family members in Boston and Honduras who shared their time, insights, and life stories with me. I hope that this book has done justice to their strength, spirit, and wisdom.

The members of Proyecto Hondureño, in Chelsea, MA, were my collaborators from start to finish. The board of directors—Elisa Enamorado, Pedro Rosales, Rubenia Bomatay, Rene Garcia, Rumina Bustillo, and Marco Antonio Velazquez—gave me the vote of confidence I needed to launch my research. Angel "Tito" Mesa and Isabel Lopez, the directors of Proyecto, facilitated my connection with the Honduran community by promoting me as their partner in solidarity. They are dear friends, mentors, and role models in the struggle for immigrant rights.

Isabel Lopez accompanied me to Honduras, graciously brought me into her own network of family and kin, and assisted me with interviews. Lidia Lopez-Murcia opened her home to me, treated me like family, and introduced me to the culinary delights of Honduras. Pedro Brizuela organized my visit with students at the Universidad Autonomo de Honduras-San Pedro Sula. I would also like to thank Octaviano Lopez-Murcia, Evangelina Lopez-Murcia, Geraldina Lopez-Murcia, Luis "Tito" Colon, and Dañiel Ramirez for their gracious hospitality, generosity, and assistance while I was in San Pedro.

Boston College and the Ben Alper Family Foundation granted me dissertation fellowships which funded my research. UNESCO awarded me a fellowship to participate in the 2003 International Sociological Association PhD Methods Laboratory. Participants in the laboratory—Michelle Hsieh, Anna Renkin, Aiste Balzekiene, Shoma Choudhury, Marcelo Medeiros, Lina Sunseri, Czarina Saloma, Cosmas Obote, Christine Inglis, Jan Fritz, Sujata Patel, Frank Jones, and Alberto Martinelli—provided me with great insights, laughter, and friendship. I would like to give special thanks to Marcelo Medeiros who helped me conceptualize transnational family mobility and who has been a great friend and support. Kathy Coll introduced me to the anthropological literature on transnationalism and gave me methodological guidance early on. Paulo Madrigal connected me with Proyecto Hondureño, and helped me in the initial recruitment phase of participants. Bart Beeson, Pedro Rosales, and Jennifer Marshall assisted me with interview transcriptions. My brother-in-law, Jim Sparks helped me construct my graphs and tables. My mom, Leone Medin, and my husband, Steve Bruner, enthusiastically proofread multiple chapter drafts. Thanks also to my colleagues at Montana State University who supported me in turning my dissertation into a book.

My dissertation committee gave me tremendous guidance and encouragement. Eve Spangler helped me maintain focus and clarity, and was always enthusiastic. Lisa Dodson mentored me through the logistical and, at times, emotional struggles implicit in field research. Sarah Babb and Peggy Levitt offered helpful feedback and wonderful support. It is difficult to express the thanks I owe my Chair, Juliet Schor. Working with her has transformed me as a person and a scholar. She walks her talk like no one else I know.

This book also benefits from the assistance of the *New Approaches in Sociology* series' editors at Routledge. Nancy A. Naples gave me great suggestions and guidance in revising my manuscript. Benjamin Holtzman was always enthusiastic, and quick to respond to my questions.

Finally, I would like to thank my friends and family. My dearest graduate school friends, Abigail Brooks and Patricia Arend, offered great insights, suggestions, laughter, and encouragement. I am blessed with a wonderful family. My uncles, aunts, cousins, in-laws, and step-parents, cheered me along the way. My Grandma, Emily Medin, offered immeasurable love and support, and was one of the first to read my completed manuscript cover to cover. My nephew Victor came into this world just as I was starting to write my dissertation. His smiling face on my computer made turning it on each morning a joy. My sister and favorite pragmatist, Anna Schmalzbauer, offered a consistent stream of love, friendship, and encouragement, and helped keep me grounded. My husband Steve is a treasure in my life. Throughout this project, his patience calmed me, his love and optimism fueled me, and his humor made laughter a cherished part of my daily routine. I dedicate this book to my parents, Leone Medin and Gary Schmalzbauer. Their unwavering love, support, and confidence in me, are the pillars on which this project was built. I am so lucky to be their daughter.

Introduction
Transnational Families and Daily Life

Rosalia and Ernesto's house in Chelsea, Massachusetts displays a mix of Honduran and American objects and images, representative of a family that is rooted economically, politically and culturally in two countries. In their living room, formica end tables covered with Honduran lace doilies stand at each end of a puffy couch protected with heavy plastic, and two wood rocking chairs, typical of homes in Central America, accompany a Rent-A-Center recliner. On the corner bookshelf, there are artificial blue and white flowers arranged in an indigenous ceramic vase perched to the side of a Boston Red Sox cap. Tourist posters of La Ceiba, Rosalia and Ernesto's hometown, along with photos of their oldest children who remain there, and a map of Honduras decorate the walls. The decorations suggest a longing for "home," a longing that is intensified by the rich aroma of pastellitos, Honduran meat-filled pastries, which fills the house.

Rosalia and Ernesto live with their three youngest children, Rosalia's sister, and temporarily with a friend and her son who have just arrived from La Ceiba. Rosalia works in a small community church. Sometimes she gets paid, and sometimes not. Ernesto, who is still without legal papers, works as a landscaper in the summer and a maintenance man and commercial cleaner in the winter. Their youngest children now speak fluent English and attend Boston's public schools. But they too are without papers, which has the children worried that they will not be able to attend college. Although they will have spent most of their lives studying and living in the United States, they are still not eligible for in-state tuition. Life is difficult for the family financially and emotionally, but somehow they manage to make ends meet and to maintain their hope for a brighter future.

Rosalia has been in the United States for six years, and her husband and three children have been here for four and a half. She came to the United Sates on a tourist visa as part of a religious delegation sponsored by a New England church. Her family's situation in Honduras at that time was dire. She was working part time managing the upkeep of a local church while Ernesto worked as a bus driver. But even with both of them working, they were barely scraping by, and their opportunities for mobility, especially for their children, appeared severely limited. They had talked for years about making the risky trip north to the United States to seek a better future. Rosalia's church trip proved the perfect opportunity. When the religious delegation was over, Rosalia did not return to Honduras. Instead, she slipped away to the house of a Honduran friend in Boston, with whom she stayed for free while working a patchwork of jobs to save the money to bring her family across the border. With help from family and kin, within a year and a half Rosalia was able to support her husband and three youngest children's "illegal" journey to the United States.

Rosalia and Ernesto's two oldest children remain in Honduras. They make do without their mom and dad, trying to understand their parents' need to go north and the logic of bringing only the youngest children along with them who could still benefit from a U.S. education. Rosalia and Ernesto's daughter, Magda, is unemployed and their son, Franklin, drives a taxi. Franklin harbors some anger toward his parents for leaving, but remains committed to the family. On his income alone the two siblings would not be able to meet even their most basic needs. Yet, with the remittances they receive from their parents they are able to live relatively comfortably. They have paid off their debts and they recently bought a sofa for their living room, a refrigerator for the kitchen, and a television, which allows them to bond with their parents and siblings by watching the same *telenovelas*. Rosalia and Ernesto's family has not been together for six years, which breeds stress and frustration, but they try to maintain a feeling of closeness via weekly phone calls, letters, and a shared understanding, that being apart is the only way for them to get ahead.

The story of Rosalia and Ernesto is typical of many Honduran families, who due to financial hardship and limited opportunities in Honduras have chosen to transnationalize as a survival and mobility strategy, negotiating the economic opportunity structures of two nation-states to sustain themselves economically and to pursue their hopes for a better future. Although divided by thousands of miles, and by politics and culture, transnational families maintain close ties across the distance (Bryceson & Vuorela, 2002; Chavez, 1998). Transnational families vary by race, class and nation. Upper and middle class families may choose to transnationalize in order to pursue career or educational opportunities, while poor families, usually with roots in the global south, transnationalize as a means of finding work that pays a living wage (Bryceson & Vuorela, 2002; Parreñas, 2005). It is the latter family form that I am concerned about here.

Sociologists and anthropologists have focused considerable attention on contemporary transnational flows of capital, labor (Sassen, 1998) and culture (Appadurai, 1996), as well as on the ways in which communities create and maintain transnational ties (Glick Schiller & Fouron, 1998; Kearney, 1995; Levitt, 2001; Smith, 1998). Only a few, however, have studied the specific role of the family in transnational processes (See Bryceson & Vuorela, 2002; Parreñas, 2005), and fewer still have looked at how families actually function in a transnational space. In this book I address this gap in the literature by investigating how transnationalism impacts and structures daily family life, and how transnationalism functions as a survival strategy in which families use the difference in living costs between Honduras and the United States to support household consumption. I look specifically at the experience and prospects of transnational labor in the United States, the aspirations and consumption practices of transnational families, especially as they relate to the "American dream," and I explore the ways in which families negotiate their emotional and material needs while striving and surviving in a transnational space.

This is a book about homesickness, frustration, and desperation, and paradoxically about hope, struggle, and family loyalty. It is a narrative about the challenges of being poor and undocumented in America, and also about the dreams and creative ways of coping formed within poor families who are rooted in two countries. This story is much different and more nuanced than the one I set out to tell at the beginning of my research two and a half years ago. I imagined then that I would be telling the tale of the political and economic marginalization of Honduran immigrants and the barriers they face to achieving upward mobility in the United States. My analysis, I thought, would be based in the theoretical framework of segmented assimilation (See Alba & Nee, 1999). Yet, early into my field research, I realized that the story of mobility and survival was one that I could not tell from the perspective of the United States or from that of individual migrants alone, nor was it solely an economic story. The lives of the Hondurans I met were much more complex than I originally anticipated.

After only a short time working within Boston's Central American community, I learned the significance of migration as a family project. As such, I decided to analyze the experiences of individual mobility and acculturation in the context of the sophisticated transnational networks of family and kin who both support and depend on the economic earnings that migration brings. Family in this situation is not bound by the borders of the nation-state or by a national culture. Instead, family is constructed and maintained in a social field, comprised of the norms, laws, and institutions of both the United States and Honduras, and is every day deeply impacted by global economic, political, and cultural forces. The daily life stories and experiences of transnational migrants reveal how these global forces are playing themselves out on the ground, at the most local level, and in the most personal spaces.

TRANSNATIONAL MIGRATION

Transnational migration is, " . . . the process by which immigrants forge and sustain multi-stranded social relations that link together their societies of origin and settlement" (Basch, Glick Schiller & Blanc, 1994:7). The transnational pathways between migrants' home and host countries are often survival pathways for poor and unemployed workers. As Rosalia and Ernesto's situation exemplifies, transnationalism is a response to structural inequalities that make it difficult for families to sustain themselves in their country of origin. It is a means of optimizing security by maintaining a resource base in two places (Levitt, 2001), and of diversifying family income by tapping into two labor markets (Massey, 1999). Growing poverty and lack of opportunity in the global south and the dependence of families, communities, and even nation states on the economic remittances of transnational migrants working in the global north, suggests that transnationalism is not a temporary phenomenon (Levitt, 2001).

The growing scholarship on transnational migration is a response to the limitations of conventional assimilationist frameworks of immigration to explain the complex realities of individuals whose lives, in response to global capitalist forces, are rooted socially, politically, and economically in more than one nation-state (Basch, Glick Schiller & Blanc, 1994; Glick Schiller, Basch & Blanc, 1992; Levitt & Glick Schiller, 2004). Traditional immigration scholarship, using the nation-state as the hegemonic representation of identity, focuses solely on immigrant incorporation within the country of settlement. Empirical research shows that this terminology and conceptual framework no longer suffice. In the current era of global capitalism, immigrants develop networks, families, activities, affiliations, life patterns, and ideologies that span their home and host societies (Basch et al., 1994; Levitt, 2001; Parrenas, 2005). Transnationalism does not negate assimilation, but instead focuses on the *simultaneity* of assimilation and transnationalism (Levitt & Glick Schiller, 2004). It is indeed possible and common for migrants to incorporate into their host countries while maintaining close ties with home.

Transnationalism is different than, but linked to, globalization. Political, economic, and cultural globalization entails the intensification of interactions between states and societies (Hobsbawm, 1975). Whereas global processes are de-territorialized, transnational processes are rooted specifically in two or more nation-states (Kearney, 1995). Transnational migration is linked to the changing conditions of the global capitalist economy and therefore must be analyzed within the context of global relations between capital and labor (Basch et al., 1994; Guarnizo & Smith, 1998; Kearney, 1995; Mahler, 1998) and the international division of labor (See Wallerstein, 1979). Deindustrialization in the United States and disruptions of economies in the global south have increased migration to the former (Sassen, 1988, 1998). Therefore, it is specifically this current moment of capitalism as a global mode of production that makes it both necessary and possible for families from the global south to maintain ties and allegiances that span nations.

The direction and path of transnational migration is a remnant of colonial rule. Many transnational migrants are now working in the countries which once colonized their home nations or have maintained them within their sphere of economic and political influence since decolonization (Levitt, 2001). The United States has been the imperial power in Central America since the 1800s. In the two hundred plus years of U.S. influence, economic, cultural, and political ties have been formed between the two regions, spurring the development of transnational ties.

The penetration of multinational capital, specifically U.S. capital, in Central America has also encouraged migration. Once workers in Central America have joined the wage labor force, working in the export factories of multinational companies, they are more easily tapped for recruitment by employers in the United States. This recruitment is further facilitated by the ideological connections to the United States that workers develop while working in these factories (Sassen, 1988). Because the employment duration of workers, the majority of whom are women, in the export-processing zone is normally quite short, they often find themselves unemployed within a few years and still poor. This unemployed pool of workers has proven ripe for migration to the United States (Sassen, 1988).

Bounded social science concepts that conflate geographical location, culture, and identity limit the ability of researchers to understand the realities of transnational migrants in the era of contemporary capitalism. Transnationalism demands that we look beyond the notions of ethnicity, nation, and culture as geographically rooted (Basch et al., 1994; Bhabha, 1990; Gupta, 1992; Smith & Guarnizo, 1998). Transnationalism is a bi-local, multi-faceted project, "that involves practices . . . that are embodied in specific social relations established between specific people, situated in unequivocal localities, at historically determined times" (Guarnizo & Smith, 1998:11).

Transnational migrants, through their daily life practices (economic, social, and political) create social fields that cross national borders (Hirsch, 2003; Levitt & Glick Schiller, 2004). Levitt & Glick Schiller (2004), defined a social field as, "a set of multiple interlocking networks of social relationships through which ideas, practices, and resources are unequally exchanged, organized and transformed . . . Transnational social fields connect actors through direct and indirect relations across borders" (1009). Analyses of these social fields focus on the multiple localities/places in which migrants live. This suggests that one does not have to physically cross a border to live transnationally. As such, we must broaden our analytical lens to encompass those who physically cross borders as well as those who stay behind (Fouron & Glick Schiller, 2002). This conceptualization shifts the focus of migration studies from that of the immigrant experience in the host country to the interaction that occurs between those who move and those who stay behind. Actors in a transnational field are impacted by multiple institutions, laws, cultures, and norms from multiple societies.

Although transnationalism suggests a world of "nations unbound" (Basch et al., 1994) in which capital, culture, and people are bi-territorialized, the territorial and cultural unbounded-ness of transnationalism should not be interpreted to mean that transnational migrants are agents without constraint (Bryceson & Vuorela, 2002; Guarnizo & Smith, 1998; Mahler, 1998) or that borders are insignificant. Whereas international capital is unhindered in many respects by law or policy, there has not been a corresponding free-flowing globalization of labor. The nation-state continues to be a critical player in transnationalism (Levitt, DeWind & Vortec, 2003). This is yet another distinction between globalization and transnational migration. The movement of international labor is impeded by strict immigration laws and by treacherous border crossings; borders still serve to keep people in and to keep people out. Although transnational migrants often subvert borders by entering their host community without papers, they do so at great risk. And those who do successfully cross the border "illegally" face severe restrictions in their daily lives (Chavez, 1998). Similarly, the State both impacts and is impacted by the actions of transnational migrants (Levitt, DeWind & Vortec, 2003).

Transnationalism from Below

Luis Guarnizo & Michael Smith (1998) distinguished between transnationalism from above and below. *Transnationalism from above* involves the weakening of the nation state via pressures from global capital (Sassen, 1988), media (Appadurai, 1996), and global institutions like the World Trade Organization, World Bank, and International Monetary Fund (Guarnizo & Smith, 1998). *Transnationalism from below* exerts pressure from the local level. Local resistances include mass migrations, grassroots mobilizations, and ethnic nationalism (Guarnizo & Smith, 1998; Keck & Sikkink, 1998). Transnationalism from below shifts the focal point of analysis from the global to the local, the daily practices and lives of people who live within transnational spaces. Guarnizo & Smith encouraged researchers of transnationalism to focus more research at the local level in order to capture the daily life repercussions of transnational forces, as well as the ways in which the actions of individuals, families, and communities assert pressure on macro level structures and processes.

Working between the levels of transnationalism from above and below, Peggy Levitt (2001) introduced the notion of a *transnational village*. Within transnational villages migration is not necessary for membership because the participation of migrants in their home communities is so great that even non-migrants are influenced by it (Levitt, 2001). Social remittances as well as economic remittances structure transnational village life. Levitt defined social remittances as, " . . . the ideas, behaviors, and social capital that flow from receiving to sending communities . . . the tools by which ordinary individuals create global culture at the local level" (11). Through social remittances, transnational migration can alter a community's work ethic, consumer ideology, expectations, political strategies, religious institutions and identity. Social remittances "help individuals embedded in a particular context and accustomed to a particular set of identities and practices to imagine a new cartography" (Levitt, 2001:11). Even those who have never left their village are exposed to new ideas about the world. Transnational villages are forever changed by economic and social remittances, and the intimate interaction that develops between transnational migrants in the home and host community fuels the continuation of transnational practices.

Inequality is an integral part of transnational villages. Although all inhabitants are exposed to the ideas and images that are transferred from the United States, only some have access to the dollars that accompany them. This can raise expectations without providing the opportunity for everyone to reach them. Levitt concluded that transnationalism heightens class divisions within communities. Indeed, very few shift class locations during the migration process.

Gender as well as class is a crucial component of transnational migration. Patricia Pessar (1999) asserted that to best understand the intricacy of transnational migration scholars should focus more attention on the *mediating units* within globalization like gender and households. It is in households and family networks, for example, that the actual decisions regarding migration are negotiated and survival strategies are put into play (Hondagneu-Sotelo, 1994; Pessar, 1999). By focusing on gender and the household, researchers can see the way power operates at the micro level and how this influences individual experiences of migration. Seldom are households democratic units based on reciprocity (Hondagneu-Sotelo, 1994, 2001; Kibria, 1993; Pessar, 1999). To the contrary, they are often ridden with conflict and structured by unequal power relationships along gender and generational lines.

Gender and migration scholars examine these relationships as central aspects of migration (Gramsuck & Pessar, 1991; Parreñas, 2005; Pessar & Mahler, 2003). At the most basic level of human need, the family and community are the theaters of action and of survival. It is at the local level that structure and agency have the most dynamic encounter. This research heeds direction and inspiration from those who write from the perspective of transnationalism from below. I have focused my research on the family. Yet while working at the family level, I am persistently attentive to the ways in which transnationalism at the global ("from above") and community/village levels impact the daily lives of transnational migrants.

THE ROOTS OF HONDURAN MIGRATION

Transnational migration between Honduras and the United States has been shaped in large part by the intimate neo-colonial relationship between the two countries. Knowledge of Honduras' history and position within the global economy is essential to understanding contemporary Honduran migration trends. Specifically, a global historical analysis shows the direct link between Honduras' persistent poverty, debt, and dependency, and the formation of transnational families.

Honduras is the original "banana republic." Indeed, no other Central American country has been as historically dependent and submissive to U.S. capital and foreign policy. Honduras' political history is defined by the American fruit companies who have owned the majority of its productive land since the beginning of the 19th century, breeding Honduras' dependence on the export of "green gold" (bananas) (Latin America Bureau, 1985). U.S. control of Honduras' banana industry was virtually complete by 1918, at which time three companies owned 75% of all the banana lands. The largest of the companies, Standard Fruit and United Fruit, continued to buy out local landowners until they owned virtually all of northern Honduras (Euraque, 1996).

Contrary to the rest of Central America, coffee was not a major export in Honduras until the 1940s (Latin America Bureau, 1985). As such, Honduras never developed a powerful coffee-growing elite. The absence of an organized national elite prompted a political structure based primarily on the power of regional landowners and the fruit companies. Throughout most of the 20th century, the fruit companies, with strong support from the United States, had a virtual monopoly over Honduras' political and economic life. Hondurans themselves owned relatively little of their country's productive resources. So, whereas coffee production led to national development, albeit unequal, in the rest of Central America, banana production actually impeded Honduras' independent development. Development in Honduras has always been dependency-oriented. It was not until 1950, for example, that Honduras established a national currency and bank (Latin American Bureau, 1985).

The control of Honduras' productive lands by the fruit companies, combined with a weak national elite, paradoxically allowed Honduras' liberal government to institute moderate land reforms, which pacified potential peasant resistance. While the rest of Central America was under the rule of right wing dictatorships, who were aligned with the elite land-owning class, Honduras was able to implement agrarian reforms in 1962, 1972, and 1975, with the backing of a strong anti-communist peasant reformist movement (Euraque, 1996). The liberal government instituted other reforms as well, including import substitution, which protected local industry and production from foreign capital, and a minimum wage. The fruit companies did not protest these reforms, seemingly because they recognized that a semblance of stability was essential to enhancing their profits and allowing for their reign to continue.

During the era of liberal reforms, Honduras remained almost wholly under the political and economic control of the United States. Even the first labor unions in Honduras, which became legal in 1959, were ruled by the American Federation of Labor. American control was further demonstrated by the takeover of Honduras' two largest banks, Banco Atlantida and Banco de Honduras, by Chase-Manhattan in 1967.

Despite Honduras' dependency on the United States, the liberal reforms of the 1960s and 1970s, and especially the anti-communist ideology in which they were embedded, steered the country away from revolutionary upheaval, which had taken hold to its north, west, and south, in Guatemala, Nicaragua, and El Salvador, to a reform-based society supervised by the military (Euraque, 1996).

Although having enjoyed relative political stability, Honduras has perpetually been the poorest country in all of Central America, and the most vulnerable to imperialist mandate. This paradoxical mix of poverty and stability, combined with its long history of dependence on the United States, and its ideal geographic location, made Honduras the obvious choice by the United States for use as a counter-insurgency base in the 1980s, when civil wars were raging in Nicaragua, El Salvador, and Guatemala. During the Reagan era, Honduras went from being first and foremost a banana republic to being a pentagon republic (Chomsky, 1985). U.S. aid to Honduras doubled in 1980 as the United States began to set up training camps and build air bases along the Honduran borders with El Salvador and Nicaragua. In 1981 Honduras became the base from which the United States launched the Nicaraguan Contra War. By 1985, there were so many joint U.S.-Honduran military exercises going on that Honduras seemed an occupied country (Latin American Bureau, 1985).

Honduran President Cordovo, along with Colonel Alvarez, leader of the Honduran military in the 1980s, and John Negroponte, US ambassador and "man in charge" of the Contra war, used whatever means necessary to enforce Honduras' National Security Doctrine, a staunchly anti-communist platform adopted from other Latin American countries. As a result, during the 1980s, repression and human rights violations, including disappearances, torture, and extra-judicial killings were commonplace in Honduras. The majority of the doctrine's victims came from popular and political organizations, but fear was widespread. The combination of fear, violence, and persistent poverty prompted the first significant wave of Honduran migration to the United States.

Although the large-scale civil wars in Central America have since ceased, and the U.S. military is no longer a prominent presence in Honduras, wounds from the era continue to fester, especially among the poor. A culture of violence persists. Drugs, a central but less publicized component of the covert wars in Central America (Scott & Marshall, 1991), have become pervasive in Honduran cities. As has been the case in inner cities in the United States and around the world, drugs have intensified violence, especially among the young. San Pedro Sula and Tegucigalpa are now two of the most gang-infested cities in all of the Americas. While I was in San Pedro Sula in 2003, my Honduran hosts would not let me set foot in or near the city center after dark, because the risk of violence was too great.

Honduras continues to be among the poorest countries in the western hemisphere, with over half the population living in abject poverty (United Nations Human Development Report, 2003). Perhaps only Haiti is poorer. Unemployment is high, wages are low, and the nation's social safety net has been withered by economic austerity measures imposed by the Honduran government and international lending agencies. 64.5% of Honduran households are poor, defined as not having enough money to afford the basic food basket. In rural areas the number is even higher, at 73%. 48% of Hondurans live in extreme poverty (Instituto Nacional de Estadistica- Honduras, 2003).

In 1998 Hurricane Mitch struck Honduras' northern coast causing major, perhaps irreparable damage to its already weak economy and infrastructure. According to the Honduran federal government, Hurricane Mitch, which also wreaked havoc in Nicaragua and El Salvador, killed 7,000 Hondurans, injured many more, and caused approximately $3 billion in damage (United States Geological Survey, 2003). It destroyed many of Honduras' banana fields, motivating multinational fruit companies to close some of their plantations and production sites. Many Hondurans lost their jobs. Post-Mitch, the Honduran formal economic sector barely exists. The informal economy is a place to which many people turn for their livelihood, but wages and earnings there are very low. Even the select few who work in the *maquiladoras* or who have entry-level professional positions do not make a living wage.

Because of the weak state of the Honduran economy, it is common that families with the means to support migration send their member(s) with the highest wage earning potential to the United States with the hope that they will be able to remit their surplus earnings. According to the Inter-American Development Bank (2001), Honduran migrants in the United States remit a total of $500 million/year, which is more than Honduras earns from the export of bananas, coffee, or seafood. It is not an exaggeration to say that remittances are a pillar of the Honduran economy and a necessity for a growing number of Honduran families and communities.

It is in this global historical context that transnational migration between the United States and Honduras emerged and has been perpetuated. Hondurans migrate to the United States because there are strong historical ties, both economic and ideological, between the two countries, and because growing social networks of Hondurans and economic demand in the United States, facilitate the immigration process. As a result of Honduras' persistent poverty and debt, transnationalism has become a survival and mobility strategy at the national, community, and family levels. Unless there is a radical transformation of the Honduran economy, which would imply an economic transformation at the global level, transnational migration between Honduras and the United States is likely to continue.

METHODOLOGY AND DESCRIPTION OF FIELD SITES

The data for this book are drawn from a multi-method two-year, two-country study. The research was guided by a grounded theory approach

(Charmuz, 2000; Glaser & Strauss, 1967) in which I gathered and analyzed data simultaneously, and continuously checked and revised the research process as new theoretical ideas and questions emerged. The research is qualitative, consisting "of a set of interpretive, material practices" that aim to make the world of the transnational family "visible" (Denzin & Lincoln, 2000:3). Using observation, time diaries, interviews, and interpretive focus groups, I immersed myself in the world of my respondents, trying to understand the transnational family from the perspective and experience of the families themselves. I was guided in my research by an overarching philosophy of flexibility in gathering data about my participants' lives. Because work/family situations can be uniquely complex when people are living under severe economic constraints, I did everything possible to adapt to my subjects' time needs throughout the research process.

I did the bulk of my field research between 2001 and 2003 in Chelsea, Massachusetts, which is a working class borough on the eastern rim of Boston. Since the 1980s Chelsea has been an enclave of the poorest and most recent immigrants to Boston, the majority from Central America and Mexico. According to the 2000 census, Chelsea is 48% Latino, but most Latino organizations in Boston estimate the fraction to be much higher. The discrepancy is due to the large number of undocumented immigrants who live there and were not represented in the census.

Although Chelsea is predominantly Central American, East Asian and African immigrants also reside there. In most stores you can find ginseng and African flat breads along with shelves of black beans, rice, and other Latin American products. Much of the housing in Chelsea is decrepit and rents are relatively cheap, which makes it a logical first stop for immigrants who come to Boston. According to the 2000 census, the per capita income in Chelsea is only $14,628/year. Although Chelsea is poor, a smattering of Central American restaurants and bakeries signify the presence of an emerging immigrant entrepreneurial class. Chelsea's ideal location on the Boston waterfront and its preserved town center, suggests that in the future, gentrification, which is already beginning, could displace the immigrant community.

I began this research with a year of participant observation at Proyecto Hondureño, a Honduran community organization in Chelsea. Proyecto Hondureño is a volunteer-based organization that was organized in January 2000 to confront the challenging political and economic issues facing Chelsea's rapidly growing Honduran community. Their mission is to promote self-sufficiency and civic participation by conducting educational activities and political actions that lead to social change. They also provide low-cost or free services to help Hondurans negotiate the logistical intricacies of the migration process. Many migrants, especially those without papers, go to Proyecto Hondureño to seek advice instead of going to a lawyer or public official. Seven days a week, there is a constant flow of people in and out of Proyecto's office.

Through out the process of this research I employed active member observation in the office and meeting places of Proyecto Hondureño. I initiated my data collection by presenting my research proposal to the organization's board. I listened to their feedback and answered their questions. They then granted me the permission and support to move the project forward, and gave me an unsolicited promise that they would be collaborators through out. I in turn promised to keep them abreast of my findings and to share my data with them for use in fundraising proposals and organizational development.

While doing participant observation at Proyecto Hondureño, I translated documents from Spanish to English, helped people apply for Temporary Protected Status, or a change in migration status, and attended local cultural events and political rallies. I participated with the organization in a major janitorial strike in Boston, as well as in a living wage campaign at a local university. I also worked with the organization on the campaign for immigrant Amnesty and I helped organize workers' rights education seminars. During all of this, I took extensive field notes. Following a constructivist approach (Lincoln & Guba, 2000) I derived the themes that guided the next phases of research from analyses of these notes.

By the end of my first year working at Proyecto Hondureño, I felt I had gained the trust of the community. In addition to the close working relationship I had developed with several colleagues, acquaintances I had made in the community began to reach out to me. I came to recognize people on the streets, the buses, and the subway. But perhaps most importantly, people who regularly came into the office began to open up to me about their lives, their struggles, and their hopes and fears about the future.

During my second year of data gathering, I recruited thirty-four Honduran transnational migrants to maintain time diaries detailed accounts of a week in the life of respondents- and to do in-depth semi-structured interviews. I could not have successfully recruited these participants without having built a solid base of trust within the community. My research overlapped with the events of September 11 and the immigrant backlash which ensued, which meant I was gathering data amidst a "culture of fear" in which immigrants, especially the undocumented, felt vulnerable to arrest and deportation. Because of the precarious and insecure daily lives of Honduran transmigrants a random sample was not feasible. Instead, I found it necessary to use purposive sampling which seeks out places where and people for whom the phenomenon under study is currently happening (Charmaz, 2000). I used Proyecto Hondureño as my recruitment base.

My time diary and interview participants were men and women, both documented and undocumented, who are the financial caretakers for family in Honduras and who had been in the United States for at least two years. All but three of them are parents. I built my U.S. sample using a snowball technique in which I asked participants to recommend other Hondurans who met the criteria for participation.

As the second component of my research I assisted the participants in the maintenance of one-week time diaries in which they logged their daily activities. I theorized that by capturing how men and women structure their days, and more specifically how they distribute their time and energy, I could better understand their daily life patterns, especially in terms of work/family balance.

I managed the diaries with a phone recall. Every day at the same time (if possible) for one week I called the participant and we spent ten to fifteen minutes talking through the last twenty-four hours of his or her day. In each daily recall, participants reported on the time they had spent in paid labor, commuting, carework, personal care, personal and family leisure, communication with Honduras, and educational and organizational activities. At the end of the daily diary I asked them if they had to interrupt any of their daily activities to care for a family member. I also asked them to detail any communication they had had with Honduras.

The time diaries served several important purposes, a few of which I foresaw and others that I never anticipated. As I had hoped, the diaries provided detailed data on the daily rituals of Honduran transnational migrants and on how gender structures their time use. In addition, and to my surprise, they provided me with a much deeper understanding of the daily realities of transnational migrants than participant observation or interviews alone could have ever done. The diaries gave me an actual glimpse into the most basic yet essential activities that structure migrants' lives. Collecting the time diary data also facilitated connections with my respondents. In addition to documenting time use, the phone recalls often segued into discussion of issues such as life in America, World Cup soccer, housework, the best Central American restaurants in Boston, work challenges, Boston and Chelsea public schools, and longings for home. Sometimes my participants shared jokes with me and sometimes they confessed that they were really down, that it had been a terrible day. By the end of a week of phone conversations I felt like I was getting to know the participants, and they seemed everyday more comfortable with me. This proved especially beneficial for the follow-up in-depth interview, as we were already at ease with, and had a basic understanding of, each other.

Although the diary methodology was extremely valuable in terms of capturing the rhythm and routine of daily life, it was also challenging. The diaries and phone recalls made me painfully aware of my privileged middle class assumptions about communication technology and the rituals of daily life. For example, voice mail and answering machines are a rarity in the Honduran community. Not only was it difficult to leave messages for participants but it was also too much to expect them to feel comfortable leaving a message for me if, for example, they had to cancel the day's appointment. Even putting my voice mail message in Spanish did little to facilitate the process. Also, many, especially the men, are here without family, and live with several others, most of whom they are not related and may even be strangers. I learned early on that leaving messages with an apartment mate is impractical, as there is no incentive for the message to be relayed. I quickly established the rule that the only sure communication is direct communication.

In addition to communication barriers, I was confronted with many scheduling challenges. Most transnational migrants do not have control over their work schedules, nor do they work set hours. One day they may work from 8am-5pm and the next day they are made to work until 8pm. Many work two or three jobs, and so they must balance a few unpredictable schedules. Those who bear heavy caretaking burdens in addition to their work responsibilities have the most hectic lives. It was therefore difficult to maintain a standard time to do the phone recalls. There were many times I got up to do a phone interview at 2am, 3am, or 6am, because those were the only times the person was free to talk.

The hardships implicit in a life of poverty presented other barriers to this methodology. Living on the economic edge means that it is not unusual for transmigrants to have their phones disconnected because they cannot afford to pay the bill. I have several time diaries that sit in my files incomplete because halfway through the week's session the participant's phone was cut off. A few of these participants got back to me at a later time apologetic about the disruption and eager to resume, but others slipped away. A few of my participants were evicted from their apartments during the course of our data collection week or had to make a sudden move to get out of an unhealthy or dangerous living environment. I learned of these incidents in two cases directly from the participant and in the others from a remaining housemate. *"Se fue ayer. No se donde esta."* "He left yesterday. I don't know where he is."

I followed the diaries with in-depth interviews, structuring each interview around variables drawn from the literature on transnationalism and the family, and themes that emerged in the time diaries. My interview questions were open-ended, allowing for in-depth discussion and the flexibility to expand the discussion to cover new topics as they arose. I did almost all of the formal interviewing in Spanish, the only exceptions being interviews with three participants who are fluent in English. Following the formal interviews, I administered a questionnaire to my respondents to get precise information on age, labor participation, level of education and literacy, number of children, household structure, years living in the United States, and rate and amount of remittances.

In addition to formal interviewing, I did many informal interviews. These interviews arose spontaneously out of my participant observation. I found these interviews and the observation to be intimately related, feeding into and off of each other.

I did the second phase of my field research in the spring of 2003 in the northern coastal region of Honduras. I chose this region because it is the primary place from which Hondurans in Chelsea have migrated. It is the heart of Central America's banana and pineapple production. Much of the region's infrastructure and productive base was destroyed by Hurricane Mitch in 1998 and still has not been rebuilt. As is true of all of Honduras, the northern coast is extremely poor, with high rates of unemployment and underemployment.

San Pedro Sula is the northern Honduran hub, the industrial center of the country, and the second largest city after the capital, Tegucigalpa. A city of 483,384 people (Instituto Nacional de Estadistica—Honduras, 2003), it is racked with poverty and violence. A large free trade zone marks the city limits. Every day buses filled with young mostly female workers make their way in and out of San Pedro's *maquiladora* sector, the major employment base in the region. Although pay is low and conditions in the factories less than satisfactory, people line up daily looking for work. In San Pedro's city center, informal vendors line the streets and gang graffiti marks many buildings. Homeless adults and children begging for money are juxtaposed against the city's elite who make their way through the streets in large sports utility vehicles and expensive cars with shaded windows. Guards armed with machine guns stand outside all banks, international hotels, and upscale restaurants. San Pedro is a bastion of despair, crime, and inequality, a city of gated communities and some of the poorest barrios in all of Central America.

In Honduras, I interviewed twelve family members of my Massachusetts respondents and six others whose family ties had been severed. My interviews in Honduras centered on how the migration of family member(s) has affected their families, the labor participation and education background of the family members who have stayed in Honduras, the role that economic remittances play in their daily lives, the images they have of their family member(s) lives in the United States, and their hopes and fears for the future.

In addition to the interviews in Honduras I spent extensive unstructured time with family members, thirty in all, sharing in meals, watching *telenovelas,* soap operas, and talking informally. One family hosted me in their home for a week. The time I spent with this family provided me a unique opportunity to observe day-to-day life, which lent itself to comparisons with the lives of their family members in Boston. I drew directly from this data in my analysis of transnational care networks and the influence of consumerism within transnational families, and indirectly in my analysis of labor mobility and time use.

For the final phase of this research I returned to the United States and recruited twenty-five Honduran transnational migrants who had not participated in the care diaries and interviews to participate in two interpretive focus groups (one group of 12 and one of 13), in which a Honduran community leader and I facilitated discussion around the major themes that emerged in my data. Interpretive focus groups address the well documented complexities and difficulties of academics doing research within marginalized populations, especially populations with a history of interrogation and a survival-based habit of coding or hiding information (Dodson & Schmalzbauer, forthcoming). The point of interpretive focus groups is to ease these difficulties by breaking through coded speech and shifting the analytical role of the "expert" from the academy to the community. Essentially interpretive focus groups seek a communitarian approach to analysis and *multivocal* representation of the meaning of data (Christians, 2000). The focus groups sharpened and deepened my understanding of my interview data. They were especially helpful in unraveling the relationship between transnational migrants and the American dream which I present in chapter three.

I did the bulk of this research in Spanish. I, or another fluent Spanish speaker, transcribed and translated all of the interviews and time diaries. The names that appear in this manuscript are pseudonyms.

OUTLINE OF THE BOOK

In this book I explore the daily lives of transnational migrants in the United States and their families in Honduras, by delving into their experiences of work and family, consumption and the American dream, economic mobility, and transnational care. I intend to show the ways in which families relate to political, economic, and cultural forces, and how they are coping with and responding to structural limitations in their lives.

In the first chapter I analyze the socioeconomic mobility of Hondurans living and working in Massachusetts. Specifically, chapter one identifies the barriers that are preventing transnational migrants from moving up the socioeconomic ladder, and it explores how these barriers impact individual and family well-being. Chapter One uses interview and ethnographic data to suggest certain structural changes that would better the lives of transnational families. Chapter Two explores the strategies of economic and emotional care that transnational families employ. This chapter starts with a discussion of how poor transnational families utilize alternative family structures and ideologies for their maintenance, then moves into an analysis of the role of economic remittances. Drawing from the literatures on transnationalism, family, and carework, it offers a gendered analysis of transnational family structure and experience, and reveals how transnational families function economically and emotionally. The goal of chapter two is to give the reader a sense of the basic structure, strategies, and challenges faced by transnational families. Chapter Three delves deeper into daily family life, drawing on time-diary data to analyze time use among Hondurans in the United States. This chapter pays special attention to the gendered dimensions of work/family relationships. Chapter Four looks at individual and familial aspirations, the role of consumerism and capitalist ideology in the family, and the ways in which families construct status in a transnational space. It also analyzes the relationship that exists between transnational families and the American dream. I conclude with a discussion of the theoretical and policy implications of transnational families, and suggestions for future studies. It is my hope that by the time the last page is turned, the reader will have a deeper understanding of the human side of globalization and transnationalism, and especially of how the lives of individuals and families are structured by global inequality and the transnational processes which flow from it.

Chapter One
Surviving in the Margins, Struggling to Move up

SEPTEMBER 30, 2002

It is a beautiful fall day in Chelsea, the Central American hub of the Boston metro area. The sidewalks are bustling and rhythmic salsa music can be heard from the windows of passing cars. A vender is selling cassette tapes and compact disks outside a popular *taqueria,* taco restaurant, while another peddles luggage from the curb in front of a money-transfer service. In Tito's bakery, a neighborhood hotspot, every table is full; there are more men than women, many who look like they just finished working the night shift. Everyone is speaking Spanish. It is a Monday, a typical work and school day in the United States, yet the streets are full. In Chelsea, unemployment is high and few workers keep a nine to five schedule. The neighborhood keeps its own rhythm.

The time I have spent in Chelsea volunteering at an immigrant rights and service organization has complicated my view of a strike effort planned for this Monday afternoon. Boston janitors, the majority of whom are undocumented immigrants from Central America, Mexico, and the Caribbean, are scheduled to strike in demand of full-time work, a living wage, and health benefits. The janitors, both men and women, clean Boston's largest and most prestigious office buildings, as well as several colleges and universities. Most clean during the night, invisible to the managers, executives, lawyers, and students who benefit from their labor. The majority work part-time and are denied health benefits and paid sick and vacation time. Many work other part-time jobs to make ends meet. I support the strike, and yet, I am deeply concerned. I wonder how this work force, the majority poverty-stricken and without a social or family safety net, will be able to stay strong for more than a day or so without full pay, especially when there is a large, surplus labor pool of unemployed immigrants who are ready to step in to take their places.

I have just finished translating a letter from the Immigration Naturalization Service for Jesus and Isabel, a poor Honduran couple. The letter states that Jesus has been denied Temporary Protected Status. They are distraught, Jesus once again having been refused a legal work permit. Jesus has been in the United States for several years and still does not have a steady job. Isabel has recently joined him from Honduras. She is tired and a bit disoriented after her long journey by foot and by bus. They are broke, and yet they tell me that they must send money "home" to Isabel's mom who is taking care of their children. I am wearing a "Justice for Janitor's t-shirt," and they ask me about the strike. They tell me that they have heard the cleaning company will be hiring replacement workers and that they are going to go sign up. I try to dissuade them from breaking the strike, but my words lack conviction. I know that Jesus and Isabel's situation is desperate. I find it difficult to tell them that they should not take work that will help them and their family.

Later, I show up at the strike headquarters. I have volunteered as a Spanish translator to pass on information to the Spanish-speaking workers about how the strike will proceed. There I meet up with Angelica, the lead worker/organizer of the building to which I've been assigned. We organize our fliers and pickets and head to our site. Angelica is strong and optimistic, but calm. When the first worker arrives, she tells us that she wants to enter the building; that she needs to go to work. Her name is Maria and she is from El Salvador. She has a heart ailment and has to take medicine daily, medicine that she cannot afford if she misses even one paycheck. She supports two children in El Salvador and she cannot afford to risk losing her job. Angelica, who is a co-worker of Maria's, remains calm. She says that she is not going to force her to join the picket line. Angelica takes Maria's hand and she walks with her and talks with her. I imagine that Angelica is telling Maria that if the workers, all the workers, don't take this risk, that they will never rise above their poverty, that this strike is the key to their economic mobility. When they return from their walk, Maria is wearing a purple "Jobs with Justice- American dream" t-shirt. Finding resolve in solidarity with the other workers, many who have life circumstances similar to her own, she does not enter the building. Instead, she picks up a picket sign.

Maria's desire to cross the picket line, as well as Jesus and Isabel's yearning to step in as replacement workers, speaks volumes about the dire economic realities facing transnational migrants. The picket line represents the boundary between the bare survival and potential economic mobility of transnational workers and their families, and the sacrifice and risk entailed in trying to achieve either or both. Without a successful strike, Maria will continue to live on the edge. She will not receive a living wage or health benefits or a vacation, and she will have to continue piecing together jobs. If Isabel and Jesus do not step in as replacement workers, they may have to go another month, or two, or three, without being able to send sufficient money to their children. Not only they, but also their family will suffer the consequences of their decision. Indeed, worker solidarity is difficult to nourish and mobility strategies hard to develop and follow when workers' job opportunities are limited and their caretaking responsibilities extend so far and wide. For just about every migrant worker, there is a family "back home" depending on financial remittances for their survival.

In this chapter I analyze the economic mobility opportunities and survival strategies of Honduran transnational migrants in the United States. I focus specifically on their job and income mobility and on how remittances affect the mobility potential of their families as a whole. My data show that generally income and job mobility are limited among Honduran migrants. Indeed, it seems that transnationalizing the family by sending a member(s) north to seek work is more commonly a formula for survival than for mobility, as structural inequalities keep transnational migrants trapped in the secondary sector, the low-wage, low-skill sector, of the U.S. economy (Piore, 1975, 1979; Sassen, 1998). Although personal agency, hard work, determination, and ambition, are inarguably critical components of the mobility puzzle (Borjas, 1999; Mead, 1992), my data confirm what many immigration scholars argue, that more important to one's mobility chances is the presence or absence of structural barriers and opportunities all of which are connected to one's position on the entangled race-class-gender hierarchy (Grosfoguel, 1999; Massey & Fisher, 2000; Sassen, 1988, 1998; Waters, 1999). Specifically, my data suggest that the socio-economic mobility chances of transnational migrants are most affected by: 1) the means of their incorporation into the U.S. economy; 2) their legal status; 3) their caretaking responsibilities; and 4) their education level and English-speaking capacity.

Although there is a small fraction of poor transnational migrants who have made their way up or appear on their way up the socio-economic ladder, I contend that the few who have achieved enduring job and income mobility have done so in large part because of unique structural opportunities that are not available to the majority of poor people in the United States. Indeed, in the current economic and political environment, the traditional

American dream formula offers little promise to poor families with origins in the global south. Transnational migrants typically work long hours, for low pay, in jobs that are refused by most Americans. In Boston, Latinos have the highest labor participation rates of all the city's racial-ethnic groups (Bluestone & Stevenson, 2000). Yet, they are barely scraping by. Still, many transnational migrants manage to protect enough of a surplus to send to their families in their home country. Transnational migrants are neoliberal role models in terms of their work ethic and family responsibility, yet mobility in the traditional sense eludes them. Why? This chapter attempts to answer this complex question.

THE INCORPORATION OF TRANSNATIONAL MIGRANTS INTO THE U.S. LABOR MARKET

Michael Piore (1975) asserted that capitalist economies are structured by a dual labor market with a primary and secondary sector. The primary sector, which encompasses business, finance, science, academia, and government, employs a highly skilled, high wage work force. Economic mobility within this sector is high. The secondary sector, to the contrary, demands a low-skill, low-wage labor force. The secondary sector includes low-end service and industrial workers. In the secondary sector mobility is restricted. The secondary sector has historically included the most vulnerable workers. In the United States, it has been supported by slave labor, then by the labor of "free" yet poor African Americans. As African-Americans gained some wage protection through civil rights legislation, recruitment for the secondary sector shifted to immigrants who had no legal rights or social protection (Sassen, 1988). Piore claimed that, workers who are recruited into the ranks of the secondary sector are relegated to a permanent discriminatory status because of their incapacity to negotiate with employers.

Sassen (1988) resonated with Piore, suggesting that recent changes in the structure of the U.S. economy, specifically the decline of manufacturing and the growth of the financial service industry in major U.S. cities has intensified the bifurcation of the economy and thus the exploitation of immigrant labor. The expansion of the high-end service sector has spurred the development of an accompanying low-wage service sector to cater to its needs. Thus, increasingly, poor transnational migrants are working in the same neighborhoods and urban centers as wealthy financial officers and corporate executives. The janitors I wrote about in the opening of this chapter are a prime example of this: undocumented Central Americans cleaning the offices of Boston's elite. Although operating in geographical proximity, workers in the low-end and high-end service sectors experience vastly different opportunity structures.

Honduran transnational migrants have arrived in the United States at a time when opportunities are lacking for all low-skill Americans. Over the past twenty years the American middle class has shrunk and the polarization between the rich and the poor has intensified (Harrison & Bluestone, 1988; Krugman, 1997; Newman, 1993). The United States now has the highest rate of inequality of all industrial nations in the world (Skocpol, 2000). The sharp drop in opportunities for working class Americans and the dramatic increase in disparity between rich and poor is due to several political and economic factors. First, the United States has shifted from a manufacturing to a service-based economy (Krugman, 1997; Massey & Fisher, 2000; Sassen, 1988), which has destroyed a plethora of permanent, well-paying jobs which once provided economic security and mobility opportunities for working class Americans (Newman, 1993; Portes & Zhou, 1993; Wilson, 1996). Second, the United States has seen a sharp increase in temporary work and sub-contracting (Piven, 2001). Whereas the wages of the American elite have sky-rocketed, the middle and working classes struggle to find full-time, permanent work that both pays well and offers basic benefits. And third, with the decline in the manufacturing-based economy, capital has ascended and labor has weakened (Sassen, 1988). Labor union membership is at its lowest level since the 1930s (Brecher, 1997).

While the bifurcation of the U.S. economy has made it increasingly more difficult for the poor and working-class to achieve upward economic mobility, politicians, democrats and republicans alike, commonly cite the culture and behavior of the poor as the reasons for their economic misfortunes. In so doing, they overlook persistent structures of inequality like low-wages, limited educational opportunities, and restricted access to basic social and human services that produce and reproduce poverty, and that can inspire behavior and modes of coping misinterpreted as cultural. *Culture of poverty* rhetoric therefore leads to misguided social policies that do not address poverty's structural roots (Edin & Lein, 1996; Schram, 2000). The resurgence of culture of poverty discourse and policy is most clear in the 1996 Personal Responsibility Act which ended entitlements for the poor, mandating work in exchange for assistance, yet did nothing to boost the minimum wage or to guarantee basic social benefits for temporary or part-time workers. At the time welfare reform went into effect, the real value of the minimum wage was 30% lower than it was at its peak in 1968 (Burch, 1997). Welfare cutbacks and work mandates have meant there are now more low-wage workers looking for jobs. This increase in supply has increased downward pressure on wages. As a result of the persistent low-wages and lack of government assistance for the poor, the number of working poor in America has grown (Newman, 1999).

Transnational migrants, especially the undocumented, are the most economically vulnerable and politically powerless of all low-wage workers in the United States (Piore, 1979; Sassen, 1988). Honduran migrants often arrive in the United States without legal working papers, speaking no English, and having little money. Many arrive in debt to the family and kin who helped fund their journey. Like most transnational migrants from the global south, they come to the United States to work, and the work they can find is almost always in the secondary sector. This means they must do hard labor for minimum wage. Most transnational migrants have little choice but to accept the work presented them. This work, most of which is temporary, is commonly found in factories, agriculture, the hospitality industry, the care industry (hospitals, private homes, and nursing homes) and commercial cleaning. The median wage of my respondents is $10/hour, and few earn far above a living wage, which is estimated to be $11.50/hour in the Boston metro area.

The hourly wages of my respondents range from $2.50 an hour to $20 an hour, the majority hovering right above or below $10 an hour. All but three earn less than $15 an hour. Wages alone do not paint a full picture of transnational migrants' socioeconomic struggles. It is the combination of low wages, variance in work hours, low opportunities, family and kin obligations, migration-related debt, and job insecurity that presents the largest challenge to well being. The testimonies that follow highlight the complexities of transnational migrants' economic struggles.

David is typical of Honduran transnational migrants. He comes from a working class family in a poor but bustling suburb of San Pedro Sula. He is the oldest of seven children. He is married and the father of two small children. He received a high school diploma from a public school, but was never able to find work that adequately supported his family. Therefore, in 1999, after many serious discussions with his wife and mother, David decided to make the long trip to the United States, crossing the border without papers to join his father and brother, who had both been working without permits for a few years.

> I remember I got to Chelsea on a Wednesday morning. I slept, rested, saw my brother, we talked and everything and then my dad asked me, do you want to go to work? That's why I came I said. Well come on

Surviving in the Margins, Struggling to Move up 25

then, I'll take you to see if you can work. And like I said, I was lucky, because the next day they put me to work. My dad took me to a work agency and said, give me your information and everything and go there in the morning. So in the morning I went with my dad who was already working there, and they sent me to work. I worked unloading the watermelons, vegetables, and potatoes.... They paid me $6 an hour.

Transnational migrants, like David and his father, often find their first jobs in the United States through a temporary employment agency. Factories and companies contract with temporary agencies to fill their lowest skill, lowest wage jobs. The companies pay the agency an hourly wage instead of paying the workers directly. The agency then pays the temporary workers a cut of the wage they receive from the company. Temporary work is unstable; workers report working one day, but not the next. Most workers who utilize the agencies are newly arrived, undocumented and often not plugged into a network that can help them find something better. Temporary work is considered by transnational migrants to be on the bottom of the job barrel. Omar, who now has Temporary Protected Status and currently works as a maintenance man for a housing project, told of his first years in Boston working for a temporary agency.

> When I came to Boston I didn't really know anyone here. So I started working at one of those offices where they send people to work, a temp agency; an agency where you arrive each day to go to one place or another. They would send me ... sometimes to a printer's shop where they print up fliers and things like that. I got paid by the people at the agency who sent me there. And the print shop paid them. For example, we took home $6/hr, and the shop paid the agency $12/hr. So, the agency got $6 that should have been ours. A rip off.... I worked in a ton of factories sometimes for one week, two weeks, three weeks. The work is temporary. When there's a lot of work they hire a lot of people, but when there isn't a lot of work you get nothing. I have worked in a lot of different places, cleaning, in a bakery, in factories. The work that lasted the longest was for six months. Sometimes the agency just gave me work for two or three days. Sometimes I only had work for one day, and the next day nothing.

Temporary agencies often supply commercial agriculture projects with migrant labor. Like other temporary work, commercial agriculture is known for its low pay and strenuous and often dangerous working environment (Chavez, 1998). Four of my respondents worked in commercial agriculture in Florida and California when they first arrived in the United States. Diego, for example, came to the United States in 1987 and immediately began picking garlic, onions, tomatoes, cucumbers, and cherries. He was paid approximately $2 an hour, the wage depended on how much he picked. He had to pay $5 a day for transportation to the work site, and there were "those terrible days" when he didn't earn enough to pay his transportation. He worked in agriculture in California for four years and his salary never improved. He finally was able to borrow some money from a relative and move to Boston where he found temporary factory work. Diego told me that he thought he was rich when he found out that he would be making $7 an hour at the factory. Three of my other respondents found their first jobs working in agriculture in New England tending to flowers and maintaining orchards and fields. They claim the work was "back breaking," the wages low, and the commute to the work site long. None endured in the industry for very long. As soon as they were able they took work elsewhere.

As the prevalence of temporary agencies indicates, few transnational migrants are able to secure a stable job upon their arrival. Indeed, there are many who never find stable employment. Most, especially those without legal work permits lose jobs because of lay-offs, health problems, caretaking obligations, or they leave out of fear that their undocumented status will be discovered and they will be deported. Ensuing job shifts tend to be horizontal or downward and wage increases are rare. In addition to being low-wage and unstable, most jobs available to transnational migrants require physical labor and have difficult work schedules and conditions.

Martin has been in the United States since the early 1990s, and has had Temporary Protected Status since 1999. He has a seventh grade Honduran education and speaks very limited English. He comes from a poor *campesino* family, and he supports his elderly parents who are still in Honduras. Since his arrival twelve years ago, Martin has held a variety of low-wage jobs. Currently he is a janitor for a major Boston university and was a participant in the Justice for Janitors strike in 2002. After ten years in the United States he told me he has only $40 in the bank.

> Well, I worked at Howard Johnson, the hotel in Boston. I was a dishwasher in '93. I also worked construction. I've had a lot of jobs. I washed cars. I worked in a restaurant in Lynn for 7 months. And there is the job I have now at the university. The job I have now is the best I think because, well, the salary is more normal. It's $10 an hour. But I work the last shift, from 10–6 in the morning. It's the tiredness that's so bad. Lack of sleep destroys people. And I mean the salary for me . . . well, it can't be right. It should be at least $12.

Surviving in the Margins, Struggling to Move up

Ernesto arrived in the United States in 1998. He has just received Temporary Protected Status. Currently he is working through a temporary agency in a factory outside of Boston. He makes $7.50/hr. Chronic back problems make it difficult for him to do physical labor, yet that is the only kind of work he has been able to find since coming to the United States.

> I've worked in construction. I've worked making shirts. The first place I worked when I came here was in a sewing factory. I worked from six in the afternoon to six in the morning six days a week, and I got paid $400 every fifteen days. That's about $6.25 an hour. That was in 1998. It was an ok job but I didn't make enough to pay the rent and send money to my family, so I left. I started working a different construction job. Things were different there because I was making $12/hr, but the job was really difficult. We spent a lot of time in the sun and I had a lot of back pain. The sun really killed you. We didn't get any benefits. They paid us in cash.

Edith has no papers. She has been in the United States for ten years, and still makes less than $10/hour. She has severe back problems, a result she told me, of years of physical labor that involved a lot of lifting. She is constantly on the look out for work that does not entail standing for long periods or having to lift or carry heavy items.

> I've done different things. I have worked in a printing company, in meat, in eggs, in packing plants, cleaning in a factory . . . . When I started they paid $5.25. That was about ten years ago. Now it's $6.75. I guess on the egg farm I did make $7. Because of my health, the job I have now isn't too bad, because I don't have to lift heavy objects and I get to be seated. Before I had to lift boxes of thirty dozen eggs.

Omar's story is similar.

> The work I do is very tough. It's work in which I have to lift heavy boxes. I'm always tired and the pay is terrible, $7.50/hr. In a year the salary hasn't changed. I started here temporarily with $7.50, but it still hasn't changed. I tried speaking to the manager, with my supervisor, to see if she'd help me with a raise since I have four children. I also have many debts and $7.50 is a bad wage. But she say's because of the recession she can't do anything. And if I lose this job I may not find work somewhere else.

Ramon considers himself lucky. He came to the United States in the mid 1980s and qualified for the amnesty program of 1986. He is now a

U.S. resident and can work and travel legally. He has worked a variety of jobs since arriving in Boston, the majority of which have been by temporary contract. Although he speaks no English and has little education, he has recently secured what he feels is a good job in a meat packing plant. He hopes that this job will offer him some stability. Even though he has legal work papers, his work life has been a roller coaster of short-lived hope followed by long bouts of frustration.

> The first job I had was . . . in a tomato factory, two weeks in '89, around June. I got here to Chelsea in May of '89. After the two weeks there, I switched to another job in another factory. Then I got a license to work with asbestos and I worked with asbestos for four years. The salary was good, but there weren't any benefits. I was making $22/hr. The bad thing was though that we worked by contract, so out of two months we only worked one sometimes. It wasn't stable, not stable at all. After working with asbestos, I worked in a bakery. It was $7/hr. I was there for two years. I only got to making $8.25/hr after two years. Then I left there because I got another job here in South Boston working in a fish factory. I stayed there for two years, until 2000. Then I went to where I am now. I'm happy here. Hopefully the job will last.

Historically, labor unions served to protect poor workers from the kinds of exploitative wages, dangerous work conditions, and unfair treatment, like those mentioned above. Although unions were not wholly democratic, often excluding the newest immigrant arrivals in order to protect more established immigrants from low-wage competition (Foner, 2000), they did help promote the economic security and mobility achieved by many European immigrant and American workers in the early 20th century (Aronowitz, 1998). Yet, as globalization has intensified and the manufacturing sector has declined, the strength of organized labor in the United States has diminished greatly (Aronowitz, 1998; Brecher, 1997; Massey & Fischer, 2000; Sassen, 1988). Vulnerable workers are less likely to challenge employers or the system for higher pay or better working conditions (Piven, 2001), thus labor unions and other social movements struggle to recruit members at the very time their action is needed most. Undocumented transnational migrants from the poorest countries of the global south are the most defenseless work force to date. Employers exploit this vulnerability, increasingly drawing on inequalities of race, class, gender, and citizenship in order to guarantee a low-paid and unorganized labor force (Chang, 2000; Cranford, 1998).

Surviving in the Margins, Struggling to Move up 29

The 2002 Justice for Janitors strike in Boston brought the low pay and exploitative treatment of immigrant workers into the public eye. Television and newspaper coverage made vivid the juxtaposition of their poverty and exploitation with the glitz and power of Boston's elite business and academic sectors. Those who paid attention to the media coverage were challenged to think seriously about the injustices occurring in the secondary sector of the U.S. economy and the need for more worker protection. Without union representation transnational migrant workers do not have the power to demand fair treatment from their employers.

Yet despite worker education and union outreach many transnational migrants remain hesitant to join unions. They say that trying to unionize would entail great risk of being fired or worse yet of being deported, a risk they are not willing to take. Anti-union propaganda playing on immigrant fears makes union organizing all the more difficult. Ramon has lead two union-drives in the factory where he works. Neither was successful. He says that the majority Latino work force voted against the union out of fear.

> Both times the union wanted to come in, the bosses took the employees to meetings every day to spread (anti-union) propaganda. . . . I think the union is a good thing. It gives us workers a vote. But the owners don't want it at all. They just want it their way. . . . There are a lot of Hondurans working here. The pay is not good, but not terrible either. But there is a tremendous amount of pressure in the work. The company has very strict policies . . . very strict. So a lot of us Hondurans, and there are Salvadorans and Guatemalans too, are trying to get a union. And in the last election we lost. The company threatened people. At the meetings they put a lot of things in people's heads. Now we have no choice but to keep fighting for better treatment for the workers.

Martin Angel has been working with Ramon on the union drive for the past year. He was previously a union organizer at the fruit factory in Honduras where he worked for twenty years. He says organizing immigrant workers in the United States is more difficult than organizing workers in Honduras, even though in Honduras union members often had to confront violent resistance. Although in the United States the workers do not fear violence, they do fear losing their jobs. Working is their top priority, and they do not want to risk the small bit of economic security that they have managed to build for themselves and for their families. To minimize risk, many workers, especially the undocumented, want to maintain their anonymity, thus they avoid meetings that would call attention to them. Being anonymous is the only way they feel safe.

> The reason we lost is very simple. The people voted for the company and not for us. Because in the company papers it says that if the union wins the employees won't get paid more, they won't get insurance and stuff like that. We are all Central Americans. Some don't like the union. They are just interested in working. They just want to work, that's all they want. Out of necessity they just want to work to support their families.

Women, Transnational Migration and the Division of Labor

Gender is an important factor in determining transnational migrants' incorporation into the U.S. economy. While male migrants commonly find work in factories, agriculture, maintenance, and commercial cleaning, women are likely to work in the care industry, either in private homes or in hospitals and nursing homes, human services, and also as commercial cleaners. This is not to say that women never find work in factories or agriculture. Like Edith, several of my female respondents reported having worked at jobs that required heavy lifting and/or toiling in the hot sun. Women also reported having worked doing tedious work, assembling identification tags, or small gadgets. But the most frequent kind of physical labor that female transnational migrants undertake is in the domestic or service sphere, cleaning and/or taking care of children and the elderly (Ehrenreich & Hochschild, 2002; Hondagneu-Sotelo & Avila 1997, Hondagneu-Sotelo, 2001; Parreñas, 2001).

As is true on a global scale (See Mies, 1986), female transnational migrants in the United States tend to be concentrated in the lowest paying and most insecure jobs (Chang, 2000; Cranford, 1998; Kim, 2000). Women who work as cleaners and/or caretakers in private homes are often the worst off of all workers. Yet, in spite of its low pay and unique potential for exploitation, domestic work in private homes is often attractive to undocumented women, especially those who have just arrived in the United States. This is because in a private home the chance of one's undocumented status being discovered and the worker thus being deported is low. The unfortunate trade-off for the enhanced feeling of security is that domestics regularly endure strict limitations on their freedom, as well as mistreatment by their employers (Hondagneu-Sotelo, 2001; Parreñas, 2001; Romero, 1992).

Ignacia's first job in the United States was in Beverly Hills, California. She went to California after spending six-months in an immigration jail in Texas. Upon her release, Ignacia's godmother, who migrated from Honduras

Surviving in the Margins, Struggling to Move up

in the 1970s, helped her find a domestic job in the house of a rich family. Ignacia spoke about her days in Beverly Hills with sadness and anger.

> In LA there are some places where people employ you for a little bit of money every week. Like I used to work in Beverly Hills, imagine, with all these millionaires, for $125/week. You know, having to clean this mansion for $125/week. So I was there and the people liked me a lot. But still they abused me. I was a maid in, or how do you say it, a live in. So, Monday through Saturday morning I was there. They let me have Saturday afternoon and Sunday to go where I wanted. But it was like I was a slave. I didn't have any freedom, and they make sure you know that you're not a part of them. I mean, you know, they have to trust you because you're taking care of their kids and stuff, but they don't treat you well. And all this for $125.

Francisca is seventy-two years old. She has worked as a cleaner and/or domestic since arriving in the United States over twenty years ago. She left Honduras when she was in her fifties because she could not find work there. In Honduras, everyone told her that she was too old. Her son, who had migrated to the United States, told her that in the United States even "old" women could find work. He helped her come to the United States illegally and a few years ago she received her legal papers. Even though Francisca has never stepped foot in a classroom, she had no problem finding work in the United States. But the work she has done is in the bowels of the secondary sector. Even with papers, she still makes below the minimum wage as a domestic, and her work schedule would tire someone half her age.

> I wake up at 3am six days a week. And then I'm just lying in bed, rolling around until 3:30am. At 3:30 I get up, go to the bathroom and shower, make the bed and then I'm out the door at 3:45. So I get here, and I have keys to open the house and I wake up the señora. I say señora get up, it's late. It's already 4am. And from there I go straight to the kitchen to make their food and make her lunch, and it's all ready to go. . . . I was hired to take care of the little girls, and to cook for them, but I say, how am I just going to cook for the girls? So I cook for her too . . . I work all day. I get paid $100/week.

It is also common for women to do informal entrepreneurial work to augment their low wages (Cranford, 1998; Foner, 1998). Francisca, for example, in addition to her work as a domestic, makes and sells *tamales*, *baleadas,* and *tortillas,* traditional Honduran foods, to families throughout Chelsea. She has a long list of customers whose names she has memorized because she cannot read or write. Once a month she calls or visits each of them to ask how many *tamales, tortillas,* or *baleadas* they want. It takes her a day and a half, working after her domestic job on a Thursday and Friday and a full day on Saturday, her one Saturday off a month, to prepare the goods. Then she sets out on foot to deliver them all on Sunday. She sells the *tamales* for $2 a piece, *tortillas* and *baleadas* for $1. Sometimes if someone is having a party she makes a special batch of tacos, which she sells for $2/piece. Her work never ceases, but she says, "That's how it goes. I have to save little by little, you know. I have to do all this work. I do it because I have to do it."

Like Francisca, Beatriz works informally in addition to her "official" job in human services. Every morning from June through September Beatriz gets up at 4am to make *pan de coco,* traditional Garifuna bread from Honduras' northern coast. After her day job ends, she goes with an aunt and a cousin to sell the bread in a park frequented by Honduran families. She sells the most *pan de coco* on weekend afternoons when Hondurans gather to play soccer in the park. She told me that it costs $10 to make ten pounds of bread, and she can sell it all for $60, so she makes $50 in profit. With this money she pays her monthly bills. Beatriz has been making and selling bread for three years, and expects to continue for many more to come.

Nadia also sells Honduran foods to Hondurans in her neighborhood. Unlike Francisca and Beatriz, though, Nadia does not have other employment, and she does not have papers. She is severely arthritic and lives for free in a small room in her sister's house. Her sister, who is now a resident, helped raise the money to bring her to the United States, with the hope that Nadia could get papers and medical care. So far neither has materialized. But Nadia is making some money from her informal business venture. The money she earns from her sales provide just enough for her to get by and to send a small amount to her daughter who now runs an informal restaurant in her home.

Transnational migrants are contributing on a grand scale to the U.S. economy. Analyses of the 2000 census reveal that there are between eight and twelve million undocumented immigrants who are working and paying taxes in the United States, but who, because of their undocumented status, will never draw on the social security and public services that they are helping to pay for. In spite of their contributions, their legitimacy is not recognized (Coutin, 2000). Like other migrants from the global south, Hondurans' incorporation into the secondary sector of the U.S. economy is at the crux of their poverty and limited mobility. In the next section I look at the specific variables that perpetuate their marginality, making it difficult for transnational migrants to break out of the secondary sector and thus limiting their family's mobility potential.

PERSISTENT MARGINALITY: BARRIERS TO MOBILITY

The Burden of Being Undocumented in America

Fleeing the poverty and misery that torment their families, many transnational migrants, with no hope of obtaining a visa, come to the United States without legal permit. Family and kin who are already in the United States help bring other family members north, often arranging false working papers for them and in many cases assisting them in getting their first job. But very few family and kin networks are able to secure legal papers for their poor relatives. Having undocumented status is a major barrier to mobility.

Undocumented workers live in constant fear of being fired or worse yet of being deported (Chavez, 1998; Coutin, 2000; Mahler, 1995). Because of this they are often not able or willing to stand up for themselves in the workplace, thus having to endure work that pays a low wage and a work environment that is often unsafe and unpleasant. That many immigrant workers are undocumented is no secret. As one respondent told me, "all the bosses know that the papers are false. But they don't say anything. They need us and we need the work." The "don't ask, don't tell" policy does not erase the persistent stress that being undocumented engenders.

Julio is undocumented. He was born into a *campesino* family in a small village two hours north of Tegucigalpa. He is one of nine children. When he was fifteen he left his family to join his older brother in Chelsea. He and the group with whom he was traveling were caught while trying to cross the border. Julio spent six months in an immigration jail in Texas before his brother was finally able to bail him out and give him bus fare to Boston. The day after Julio arrived in Boston he began working in a produce factory. He has now been in the United States for seven years. He still does not have papers. Even though he is married to a Honduran who has U.S. residency and has a daughter who is a U.S. citizen, he is not able to apply for his papers without leaving the United States for three years. Because of his responsibilities as a husband and as a father, he refuses to do so. Julio was fired from his first job because he stood up to his boss in protest of the harsh treatment of and lack of respect for workers in the factory. If he had had papers, he would have stood up to his boss much earlier because he would not have been so afraid of being fired.

I was there for five years in a tomato and fruit company. It was really bad. At the beginning I was afraid that I wouldn't be able to find another job so I put up with everything they did and said. I was working ten hours a day, six days a week. And they paid a low wage. And the salary never changed. They paid $8.50 for five years. And there were no benefits. But they can do this because they know that you're an immigrant and that you don't have papers. They know that. You don't have any rights. They know that. The bosses were Italians. Very mean. Fascists. They were always yelling and forcing us to work. 'Come on let's go. Move! Move!' Very mean. The job itself wasn't that bad. To me the type of work isn't important. We are used to working hard. But how they treated us was the hard part. There wasn't any respect. And when one day I said something to the boss, they threw me out. I didn't have papers. I still don't have papers. It's very difficult.

Paula has been in the United States for five years and is undocumented. She told me she feels more vulnerable now than ever before. Since the events of September 11, the increased vigilance towards all immigrants, especially those from the global south, has prompted increased unease within the Honduran community. "It's really difficult to work without papers. Papers protect you. Because if the police or immigration arrives and says something to you or if they look at you badly, you only have to present your papers. If you don't have them they take you in. There are a lot of deportations now."

Transnational migrants and their advocates recognize the barrier to mobility and the risk that not having papers poses to them and to their families. Not having papers means that temporary work at low pay and in poor working conditions is one's only option. Low pay, especially in cities like Boston where the cost of living is high, limits the amount of money that transnational migrants are able to remit to their families, thus choking mobility opportunities and sometimes threatening family survival.

In 2000, a coalition of immigrant organizations launched a major campaign for a legal amnesty for all undocumented workers. The campaign, which had gained momentum with the support of Illinois Congressmen Luis Gutierrez, Massachusetts Senator Ted Kennedy, and Mexican President Vicente Fox, was dealt a major blow by the events and aftermath of September 11. Members of congress and even President Bush himself, who had seemingly been leaning towards support of an amnesty, immediately reversed their stance following the terrorist attacks. Although President Bush has since proposed a three-year guest worker program, nothing has concretely changed.

Tavio, a long-time leader within the Honduran community in Chelsea, told me in a 2003 interview that undocumented workers are experiencing more exploitation and hostility than ever before. The threatening political reality coupled with economic recession makes it increasingly important that amnesty be granted.

> I think the community of immigrants is facing more barriers and constraints than ever before, certainly more than when I came in the 1970s. What's changed is that there's been more radical positions taken by the people who rule this country and so there's more hostility towards immigrants, including hostility that is created through the media. The repercussion of the media portrayal of non-Americans, even though it's directed at those from the Middle East, is impacting the Honduran community. So that makes it difficult to make changes, to run a pro-immigrant political candidate, and to do a lot of things that we want and need to do to make things better for Honduran families. The laws that have been passed, like the Patriot Act, are barriers for immigrants. They single out undocumented immigrants for deportation. . . . A capitalist country like the United States sees the benefits of cheap labor, and they pass laws to insure it. The laws that have been passed since September 11 make it even more difficult for us to achieve our goals. . . . So I think the struggle for legalization, amnesty, is one of the main things that we have to continue to fight for. I think it's going to be very difficult to pass modification of the law since conservatives dominate congress. Even the people who embraced our cause before now put all attention to staying in power. But the fight for amnesty has to continue. Legalization is the biggest barrier Honduran families face.

Education and English

Honduras has an illiteracy rate of 25% (CIA World Fact Book, 2003). With the onset of structural adjustment policies in the 1990s, education, especially secondary and university education, has become almost exclusively an opportunity for the wealthy. School registration fees, in addition to costs for uniforms and textbooks, are required of public school students. Financial remittances help cover these otherwise unaffordable education expenses. My respondents in both the United States and Honduras reported that education costs are one of the primary places remittances are channeled.

Although many of the transnational second generation in Honduras are now attending school, many transnational migrants in the United States did not have educational opportunities when they were growing up. From colonial through post-colonial times, only the wealthiest of Hondurans have attended good schools and have had the opportunity to learn English. In Boston, Latinos have the lowest education levels of all ethnic groups. Only 42% of Boston Latinos have completed high school (Bluestone & Stevenson, 2000).

Francisca is typical of poor Hondurans of her generation. She cannot read or write. The oldest of nine children, she was charged with taking care of her siblings while her parents worked in the fields. When Francisca was forty years old, a doctor who worked in her town's clinic offered to help her learn to read and write. Francisca was determined to learn how to write her name, a feat she accomplished and of which she is proud. Although Francisca now has legal residency in the United States, her limited educational skills, which are a result of her family's poverty and her caretaking responsibilities, prevent her from finding work outside of the secondary sector.

> My parents never . . . well, before people never imagined that knowing to read and write was so important. Everyone had to work. My father worked in the cornfields and also growing beans and rice and taking care of the fields. My parents never put me in school. Some of my mother's other children went to school for a while but I was the oldest so I stayed home taking care of everything.

Arriving in the United States with a weak educational background makes it difficult for transnational migrants to learn to read, write, and speak English. Of the thirty-four Hondurans I interviewed in Massachusetts, only seven speak English. Three learned English in Honduras. Of these three one attended a bi-lingual high school in San Pedro Sula. The other two are Garifunas, black Hondurans from the northern coast, who speak English as well as Spanish. Of the four who learned English in the United States, two married Americans from whom they learned English and the other two were young enough when they came to the United States to attend American high school where they picked up English quickly.

Not speaking English breeds frustration and low confidence. Dañiela, who recently got Temporary Protected Status and found a job working with Latino children in a community Head Start program, told me that, "The most frustrating thing is the language. English used to be a huge fear of mine. I'm still afraid because I don't speak English. I have no confidence because I can't speak the language."

Even if workers have legal permit, their lack of English makes it difficult for them to defend themselves in the work place and in society in general. My respondents said that intimidation, frustration, and fear are common stress factors that come from not speaking English. Paulo who works as a janitor in a Boston university told me that if he and the other workers in his group could speak English the work environment would be much better.

> If I could I would study English. I know that it would benefit me and I'd be willing to sacrifice to do it. But only if it was a possibility, which it's not. If we could speak English we'd be able to relate better to our bosses. We could defend ourselves when they mistreated us. Sometimes they mistreat us because they think we've done something that we haven't, but we can't correct them. And sometimes they misinform us about things. We're all ignorant about these things because we don't speak English.

Most of my respondents, like Paulo, said that if they had the chance they would learn English, and that not speaking English is one of the largest barriers they face in this country. Yet the intense pressure on their time coupled with their limited income, and weak educational base makes learning English and going to school difficult if not impossible. English classes are expensive and they are often held in the evenings when many are working. Even for those who can afford the classes and for whom the class schedule does not conflict, housework and caretaking work often make taking classes impossible. This is especially true for women who are commonly charged with the responsibility for domestic tasks.

Dorotea came to the United States with a goal of learning English. She had basic-English classes in high school in Honduras and thought she would be fluent soon after her arrival. But financial limitations as well as household responsibilities got in the way of achieving her goal.

> Many of us don't have the opportunity to study in the United States because we work all the time. Our work impedes us. I studied English for almost two years, and I had to pay $1400. The schools here don't give aid to foreign students. And so I couldn't afford it anymore. And I had my other responsibilities, you know as the woman in the home. I know that in this country there is a lot of opportunity, but we are people that don't have anything. No one arrives in this country with money. So what can we do?

Neoliberal immigration scholars cited lack of English and education as major factors that impede mobility (Borjas, 1999; Chiswick, 1978; Mead, 1992). While my data supports this general view, it challenges neoliberal cultural explanations, which tout ethnic characteristics transferred from generation to generation as the reason for low levels of education attainment and low mobility. Borjas (1999), for example, asserted that "disadvantaged ethnic environments- where most parents may be high school dropouts or welfare recipients- imbue the children raised in those environments with characteristics that impede future socioeconomic achievement" (146). Contrary to Borjas' hypothesis, the majority of my respondents cited the education of their children as a primary goal, although one they find very difficult to achieve. They also said that they themselves want to learn English, and pride themselves in having taken steps in attempt to do so. Yet despite the value of education in the Honduran community, education and English levels are persistently low.

My data suggest that low-levels of education and English among Honduran transnational migrants are not a result of lack of ambition or vision, but a result of the social and political economic context which constrains their opportunities and choices (Mahler 1995; Portes & Rumbaut, 1996). Honduras' poverty, which is experienced as family poverty, low wages in the United States, lack of free time and surplus money to afford classes, a weak educational base, and a hostile economic and political climate for transnational migrants in the United States, equate with low English and educational attainment. While non-commercial classes are available, waiting lists are long because spaces available, especially for discounted or free classes, are far fewer than the number of people wanting to attend them. Until the severe structural constraints to education are addressed and remedied, English and skill levels among Honduran transnational migrants will remain low and mobility opportunities stifled.

Segregation

Most of my respondents work with other Latinos in secondary sector occupations and live in Latino neighborhoods. They are in large-part segregated from native-born whites as well as from African Americans, Europeans, and often African and Asian immigrants as well. On the national level, Latinos are more segregated than immigrants in general (White & Glick, 1999).

Research done by Massey & Fisher (2000) shows that racial segregation interacts with income inequality in the United States to concentrate poverty. Massey & Fisher found that changes in the social economic structures can have different effects on groups depending on their level of segregation. My data supports their thesis. Chelsea, where the majority of my respondents reside, has one of the highest isolation indexes in all of the Boston Metro area. In Chelsea, Hispanic- white segregation exceeds black-white segregation at the national level (Bluestone & Stevenson, 2000).

According to the 2000 Census, Chelsea also has one of the lowest average household incomes in Massachusetts.

William Julius Wilson (1996) acknowledged the prevalence and persistence of racial and ethnic segregation, but argued that income inequality and class segregation are at the crux of African American poverty. He thus proposed class-based strategies to counter concentrated poverty. My data suggest that class-based strategies would not address the looming problems that come with being undocumented and non-English speaking. Hondurans suffer segregation and exploitation based on race, ethnicity, and class, yet because they are not American citizens, they are disconnected from many of the class-based movements and policies that seek to support the poor and working class. Wilson's thesis does not address the complex marginalization that transnational migrants face.

Chelsea is marginalized and it is poor. Housing in Chelsea is rundown and overcrowded. Several of my respondents report problems with cockroaches and rodents. My female respondents told me that they are frightened to be out in the streets at night because street gangs dominate their neighborhood. Public transportation is limited and unreliable. The only way to get to downtown Boston from Chelsea is to take a bus across the Tobin Bridge. It is one of the only places in the Boston metro area that is not accessible by train. I rode the #111 bus on my way to and from Chelsea. The bus is commonly overcrowded with Central American workers going to and from their jobs, and often it is late or has to skip stops because there are too many people already on board. Once the bus gets across the bridge and into the city, workers have to connect to other buses or to the subway in order to get to their final destination. It took me between an hour and hour and a half to get to Chelsea from my Boston neighborhood. My respondents told me that this is an average commute. There is nothing easy about getting in and out of Chelsea. In addition, in Chelsea, public services are weak, employment opportunities few, and the high concentration of undocumented residents means that few can vote or exercise influence to change the system. Life for transnational migrants in Chelsea is life on the edge. Most must constantly negotiate an intricate survival path.

Segregation, both residential and occupational, and the poverty which accompanies it, can breed inter-ethnic tension and competition, which erodes the potential for Latino solidarity. As Sarah Mahler (1995) found in her research on undocumented Latinos in New York, Latinos often blame each other for their poverty and misfortune instead of focusing their frustration on the social structures that constrain them. Mahler's research concluded that the pressure immigrant workers have to remit surplus earnings to their families and kin back home inspires exploitation and mistreatment of Latinos by other Latinos. My data supports Mahler's findings, and it also suggests that immigrants blame each other and compete with each other because the majority of contact they have is with each other. All but four of my respondents work solely with Latino migrants. Marta who cleans airplanes at Logan airport has a typical work set-up.

> I'm working with a lot of Latinos. Yes, just Latinos. In the factory they were all Latinos. In California it was all Latinos, and where I am now, they are all Latinos. I hear there is a Puerto Rican coming but he hasn't gotten here yet. All the Latinos are from Guatemala, El Salvador, and Honduras. And there's a Mexican. So we speak Spanish, everything in Spanish.

Even North American-owned businesses often have Latinos supervising the Latino workforce. The supervisors I am told have usually been in the United States a long time and have their papers. In this sense there is a hierarchy amongst Latinos, a hierarchy in which the undocumented and most recent arrivals are on the bottom.

> We are approximately seventy to eighty people that work cleaning the university in the night. Almost all of us are Hispanics. There are workers from Colombia, from all over Central America, from Haiti, Dominican Republic and Puerto Rico. . . . Sometimes we Hispanics fight among each other. I don't know why. In our case our supervisors are Hispanics, and they don't treat us well. There are a lot of examples.
>
> —Martin, a janitor at a Boston university

> Sometimes our supervisors mistreat us. They are Hispanics too but they think that they have done enough things that they aren't like us anymore. This happens between us immigrants. Sometimes between us, we do things to stop the others from moving ahead. Can you imagine telling my boss that another compañero is working badly?
>
> —Paulo, a janitor at another Boston university

In my discussions with transnational migrants about racism and discrimination in the workplace and in their neighborhoods, the majority of my respondents told me that the only racism they had confronted was from other Latinos and from African Americans. This phenomenon is no doubt a product of the poverty-segregation interaction that Massey & Fisher

(2000) theorized. Veronica, a clerk in a Boston courthouse asserted that, "I never experienced racism against me from white persons. I always experienced racism from my own people, the blacks and Hispanics; at work, in the bus, on the train, on the street. Like in my job right now that's what I'm facing, and that's what bothers me because I say, wow, they are very ignorant people." Donaldo, a union organizer in a Boston meatpacking plant, also feels that inter-ethnic racism is common. He said, "Racism is a problem everywhere. That's a problem we have now, and not just toward person X. Even amongst Latinos there's racism. Sometimes we're the worst. There is a lot of jealously amongst us. That's the problem in the factory where I work, because it's a company where the majority is Latino. And there's a lot of jealousy and selfishness."

The intersection of poverty and segregation spurs intense competition for jobs (Wilson, 1996) and status (Mahler, 1995), which can be experienced as racism among transnational migrants. Occupational segregation keeps wages low by making it difficult for unions to organize, and by hindering migrants from learning English or building social networks with non-immigrants through which they might be able to access better jobs (Mahler, 1995). The immigration-segregation-poverty cycle perpetuates itself confining transnational migrants to the secondary sector and to marginalized immigrant neighborhoods, and therefore severely hindering opportunities for economic mobility.

Alejandro Portes (1986, 1993) and colleagues reported that residential segregation can, in certain situations, enhance the mobility opportunities of immigrant groups. They learned that although a bifurcated economy relegates many immigrants to the ranks of the secondary labor market, there are still means of increasing the opportunity structures of immigrant communities through the creation and maintenance of social networks in ethnic enclaves (Portes & Manning, 1986; Portes & Zhou, 1993). Ethnic enclaves are defined as geographically, economically, and politically delineated communities of immigrants from the same home country that operate on the basis of solidarity and reciprocity. Enclaves offer entrepreneurial and other professional opportunities through good-will loans and rotating credit schemes, on-the-job-training, advancement to supervisory positions, and employer assistance programs that can be tapped in times of personal or familial economic emergencies (Portes & Manning, 1986). The ethnic solidarity that structures these enclaves is facilitated by the following important factors: spatial concentration; the initial arrival of a moneyed, entrepreneurial class; and the replenishing of the labor pool with future refugees (Portes & Manning, 1986). Common examples of contemporary ethnic enclaves include Koreans in Los Angeles and Cubans in Miami.

The Central American community in Chelsea does not fit the ethnic solidarity model. While the majority of Cubans and Koreans entered the United States as political refugees and received a warm welcome from the U.S. government, as exemplified by access to generous public assistance and their social construction as *model minorities,* Hondurans and other Central Americans enter the country for the most part without documents, have received no social assistance from the United States government, and are often characterized as deviant. The majority of Honduran transnational migrants do not enjoy political or social security, nor do they have the resources to pursue entrepreneurial ambitions. Hondurans simply lack the human and financial capital to develop a thriving Honduran enclave. Instead, Hondurans live a segregated existence, one that breeds inter-ethnic tension and competition.

Caretaking Responsibilities

Transnational migrants demonstrate strong ties to family and kin both in the United States and Honduras. These ties are expressed in the caretaking obligations they fulfill by sending financial remittances. The family and culturally imposed mandate that they have to send money to Honduras makes it difficult to save. The pressure to remit translates into longer work hours and spending little money on their personal and immediate needs. The tradeoff is difficult to measure, as the families receiving remittances clearly benefit from the ensuing increase in financial security, material comforts, status, and opportunity for education advancement that U.S. dollars afford. Transnational migrants in the United States sacrifice their individual mobility to make life better for their families. Omar testified to the tight budgets within which transnational migrants live. "The end of this week I will have $512. I will send $300 to my country for the food for my children. The other two hundred I have to spend to fix my car, which I need to get to work. Every week it's like this. In Honduras I have my mom and my children, and they all rely on my money."

The mean amount of monthly remittances of my respondents is $242. The mean wage of this same group is $10/hour. At $10 an hour, for forty hours, my respondents are making $1600 a month before taxes. They must pay rent, and housing costs in the Boston metro area are among the highest in the nation. They must also buy food, clothes, and pay for their transportation. Because very few have health or dental insurance, an illness can send the individual and the family who depends on her/him over the edge. One of the Hondurans I met while volunteering in Chelsea complained of a terrible toothache that he had for over a week. He could not afford to go to a dentist to have it pulled and because he was undocumented he feared revealing his status to the community clinic, the one place where he might have been eligible for free care. This story is typical. Whether it is a toothache, infection, or bad bout of the flu, transnational migrants rarely can afford a doctor's visit. They send the money that remains at the end of the month after paying for life's basic costs and unexpected emergencies to Honduras.

Because transnational migrants remit their monthly surplus earnings to Honduras, they are unable to spend money on mobility enhancing strategies like taking English classes or educational training. Nor are they able to save for a move to a better apartment or to buy a home in the United States. Without an economic safety net, life is tenuous, and most every day is stressful. Maria was hesitant to join the Justice for Janitor's strike because she was terrified of the repercussions to her own health and to the well-being of her family if she missed even a day's wage. With no savings or social protection, and a family relying on remitted wages for their own survival, many workers are hesitant to join organized labor struggles or, as one respondent told me, "to make any waves what so ever." The risks are too high and the potential repercussions great.

While all of my respondents are remitting money to their families in Honduras, several of them also have major caretaking responsibilities in the United States. Women in particular testified that having to care for their children placed limitations on their ability to work outside of the home. Research that has been done on working women in the United States shows that women continue to bare a disproportionate burden for the direct caretaking of their families (Heymann, 2000; Hochschild, 1989; Schor, 1992), and that this burden of care is even heavier for poor women (Dodson, 1998; Edin & Lein, 1996). Since the welfare reform legislation of 1996 went into effect, migrants are not eligible for most forms of federal and state aid. Undocumented migrants face even stricter restrictions. Therefore transnational migrant mothers are in the most difficult work/family bind of all.

Some of my female respondents are able to ease some of their caretaking burden by tapping into caretaking networks of family or friends. Maria, for example, told me of the struggle she faced when her daughter was born with a bronchial ailment, and she had to leave her job to take care of her. Finally, a friend of Maria's who recognized Maria's economic desperation, volunteered to take care of the baby so Maria could go to work.

> I wanted to work, but with Helen I couldn't because she was ill. . . .
> One day I had to take her to the hospital because it was like she was

drowning. The doctor told me that he couldn't help her, and that I had to be with her all the time, taking care of her. So I had to quit my job, and stay home taking care of her. . . . So I was at home. . . . I didn't have a work visa or papers, but I had to find work. So a friend told me, 'I will take care of her for you. Go and work.' And I trusted my friend, and went to look for work.

Social networks of family and friends can serve as life-saving caretaking supports (Collins, 1994; Stack, 1974). But not everyone has a network that they can tap for help. Most poor transnational migrants have family and friends who are just as poor, and who have the same work and family pressures. Eva, for example, has some family in Boston, but none that can help take care of her children. Eva left her job because her work schedule conflicted with her children's school schedule and she had no one to help her. She was afraid that if she were not with her children before school that she would be accused of negligence in which case she would risk losing her children.

My baby was just going to K2. . . . I couldn't leave her standing alone waiting for the bus while I go to work. No way could I do that. So I called up my supervisor and said I'm sorry but I can't do it. I'd like to go back to that job, but I can't because of how I left. I didn't even give them two weeks notice. I feel like they betrayed me too because I asked them for help. I told my supervisor, kid's school is coming up and I need to change my hours. I told her like two or three months before school started. . . . When the time came she never had done nothing. It was too late. My kids had already started school. They had to miss school for two or three days because I couldn't take them to school. I was still trying to work out if I could find someone to take them, and I didn't find nobody. So I called them up and I said I'm sorry but my kids come first. If I leave them standing at the bus stop while I go to work, what are they going to do? They are going to call DSS on me, you know, and I can't do that. I can't afford to lose my kids.

Caretaking responsibilities pose a major barrier to the economic mobility of Honduran transnational migrants. In the United States individual mobility is often emphasized above family mobility because family is seen as a potential threat to individual gains (Mahler, 1995). Yet Honduran transnational migrants tend to put the needs of their families first, often sacrificing their own well-being to ensure the security of their children, siblings and/or elderly parents. On the U.S. side of the economic mobility equation, they are barely scraping by. They are caught in a terrible bind in that if they want to move up themselves, they must extricate themselves from their obligations to family and kin, a move that would be condemned by the Honduran community at large prompting the self-seeking individual to be ostracized and isolated (Also see Mahler, 1995).

MAKING IT IN AMERICA

The mobility story of transnational families would be incomplete without telling of the exceptions to the rule. There are examples of families who have achieved enduring mobility in all the transnational spaces the family occupies. Four of my respondents told me that they have "made it," that they struggled and sacrificed, and they achieved the American dream. What makes them different? Ignacia's story reveals several important variables that enhance a family's mobility chances.

Ignacia is the oldest of seven children. She was raised by a single mom who earned meager wages working as a vendor in the informal economy of San Pedro Sula. When Ignacia was sixteen she had a baby, and decided that the only way she could support her child and help her family was to go to the United States. Leaving her baby with her mother, she set out alone. When she was crossing the border she was caught and sent to immigration jail where she stayed for six months until her godmother bailed her out. She entered the United States in debt. Desperate, she took a job as a "live-in" for a wealthy family in Beverly Hills. At this time Ignacia had no papers, spoke no English, and had no high school degree.

After a year in Beverly Hills, Ignacia was able to pay off her debt to her godmother. She was also granted her legal papers as part of the Amnesty legislation of 1986. She then moved to Boston to marry a Dominican man whom she had met in the immigration jail and with whom she had remained in contact. The marriage was abusive. A week after the birth of her son, Ignacia's husband beat her almost to death. She ended up in a Boston hospital and was then placed in a shelter. While she was in the shelter Ignacia enrolled in English classes and then in a general education degree (GED) program. She took advantage of the shelters' extended day care hours and worked during the evenings.

Once she had saved a bit of money, a social worker helped her apply for a Section Eight housing subsidy, and she was soon able to move into her own apartment. She kept working and going to school. She learned English, and got her GED, and immediately enrolled in classes at a community college. She received a day care subsidy. Because of day care and the babysitting help of her sister who had arrived from Honduras, Ignacia was able to continue working and going to school. Aid to Families with Dependent Children (AFDC) provided her with the additional financial support that she needed to make ends meet.

Ignacia finished a two year community college program, receiving an associates' degree in Human Services, and was soon hired by the very shelter that she credits for changing her life. She remarried, had another child, and began her move up the professional ladder in her field. Ignacia now makes $40,000/year as a housing consultant for the state of Massachusetts. She and her husband own a house and are saving money for their children's college education. Ignacia is a leader in the Honduran community and she supports several grassroots development efforts in Honduras. She is also an active church member and the head of the parent's group at her children's school. She has "made it."

Through all of her struggles, Ignacia has supported her family in Honduras. Even when she barely had enough to eat herself, she sent money "home." As she began to earn a higher income she increased her assistance to her family. With her assistance her family was able to do major improvements to their home, including installation of a potable water system, a tile floor and an outdoor security wall. Because of Ignacia's remittances her daughter in Honduras was able to attend a private high school and is now one of only a few women enrolled in the best technical university in Honduras.

Ignacia visits her family every year. Each time she brings suitcases of gifts and money. She has also paid and arranged for her mother to visit Boston. When I interviewed her in Honduras, Ignacia's mother told me that she did not think she could have made it without Ignacia's help, and that she never would have dreamed that she would have a sense of security in her old age.

Ignacia's story is unique. Seldom are transnational migrants from poor families able to lift their families as well as themselves out of poverty. Ignacia's strength, hard work, sacrifice, and perseverance are indeed special. But underlying her commendable drive and sacrifice are structural elements that deserve mention. Ignacia's story is not unique because of her hard work, sacrifice, and perseverance. Perhaps she risked more, worked a bit harder, and exercised more optimism than her peers, but I do not think that Ignacia is that different than other transnational migrants I interviewed in these respects. What is most unique about Ignacia's story is the result that her hard work and sacrifice yielded.

Ignacia came to the United States when she was young, sixteen years old. She was strong, healthy, and eager to learn English and go to school. After only a year in the United States she received her papers, which allowed her to enroll in English and high school classes, to get work that paid above the minimum wage, and to qualify for AFDC. When Ignacia suffered severe abuse from her husband, she was not afraid to ask for help. She knew that as a U.S. resident she could not be deported. Her plea for help was answered and she was assigned a social worker who helped place her in a shelter, access subsidized day care, and continue with her studies. Because Ignacia was able to qualify for Section Eight housing, she was able to leave the shelter and live independently and in decency while she studied, worked, and raised her family.

Without receiving her papers, Ignacia would not have had the welfare support which enabled her to study, get a degree, and learn English, while simultaneously taking care of her children in the United States and sending money to her family in Honduras. If Ignacia would have arrived in the late nineties instead of the eighties, she would have been ineligible for AFDC, legal amnesty, Section Eight, and the student loans that helped her go to school. These structural supports have been denied those who have arrived in the last several years. I include Ignacia's story because it shows the mobility potential that transnational families would enjoy if they had basic structural supports to add to their hard work and sacrifice.

CONCLUSION

The general incorporation of transnational migrant labor, especially undocumented labor, into the secondary sector of the U.S. economy means that most transnational migrants are stuck with low wage, temporary jobs that lack benefits and other labor protections. The scars of Honduras' colonial history, the tenuous legal status of transnational migrants, as well as their lack of English, low education skills, caretaking responsibilities, and segregated existence, are all variables that perpetuate the poverty and marginalization of Hondurans in the United States. Although the money that they remit to their family and kin in Honduras does secure their survival, and in some cases enhance their educational opportunity and comfort, it is sent at great sacrifice to their individual mobility in the United States.

While the implementation of structural supports in the United States would enhance transnational families' chances for economic mobility, there still remains the enormous barrier posed by Honduras' position within the global economy, and Honduras' history of colonial and postcolonial exploitation by European and American powers. Honduras is a poor and dependent nation. Its status as one of the poorest countries in the world diminishes the mobility opportunities of most every family whose origins are within its borders. Ignacia, for example, has indeed "made it," but she still bears the burden of supporting a large family of individuals who have not had the same success. Ignacia sends home a few hundred dollars every month. In addition she sends extra money and material goods for special occasions and for emergencies. If she were to lose her job her entire family would suffer the repercussions. She provides her family a security blanket, but the blanket is stretched thin.

The only Hondurans who have sustained high economic status, security, and mobility potential across the generations are those who are descendants of Honduras' original colonial ruling class. They have inherited privilege, wealth, and power. The class hierarchy in Honduras is rigid. Walled and heavily guarded residential compounds built on hills away from the ugly poverty and desperation of the Honduran masses symbolize the feudal-like control maintained by the Honduran elite. Poor Honduran transnational families sacrifice and endure much, yet in the contemporary global system, their chances of breaking into the upper echelons of the Honduran and/or global economy are slim.

Chapter Two
The Strategies and Challenges of Transnational Care

'I haven't seen my mom in ten years. . . . She's told me about life in the United States. She says, '*mi hija* (daughter) life is hard here. Here you work like a mule. Life isn't easy. Here if you don't speak English, it's difficult to find work. And if you don't read and write they humiliate you. I've had to go through all that, which is why I'm telling you this. But I've done it for you *mi hija*. I haven't been able to bring you here to be with me because my economic situation is so bad. But one day, I promise you, we will be together again.'

—Lourdes, Portrerillos, Honduras

The economic mobility struggles of transnational migrants in the United States comprise only one component of the transnational family existence. Their paid labor in the United States is partnered with the unpaid carework of family members in Honduras. It is only by employing a transnational division of labor that family survival is insured.

In this chapter I examine the every day challenges and coping strategies of families which depend on a cross-border division of labor. I explore the ways in which these families function economically and emotionally. Fundamental to the thesis is that processes of economic globalization have had a radical impact on the structure and practices of transnational families. The concentration of capital, and therefore employment opportunities, in the north, has spurred massive migration of labor from the south (Sassen, 1998), as poor families increasingly find themselves in the position of having to decide between sinking further into poverty together and sending one or more members north to find work. The result is a growing phenomenon in which poor families, already marginalized economically and politically, who have little choice but to live apart. Their unique struggles comprise a major social problem that has been overlooked in much of the literature on both transnationalism and family. This chapter seeks to help fill the voids in these literatures, by analyzing: 1) the role of *othermothers* and kin networks in the survival strategies of transnational families, 2) the economy of the transnational family, 3) the emotional components of transnational care, and 4) the challenges to family reunification.

THE TRANSNATIONAL FAMILY

The transnational family is not a new phenomenon (Bryceson, 2002; Foner, 2000; Ueda, 1994; Wyman, 1993). Many families and communities in Europe in the 19th and early 20th century, for example, depended in large part on the financial remittances of their members who were working in America. Families stayed in touch by writing letters, and they strategized reunification, a process which was often accomplished with eventual return migration to Europe (Foner, 2000). Many who did settle in America permanently maintained strong ties to their families, and to the cultures and politics of "home." Nina Glick Schiller (1999) argued that the transnational lives of these earlier immigrant families were seldom written about, not because they did not exist, but because there was not the conceptual framework to explain the transnational spaces between nation-states in which their lives and identities evolved.

Although the transnational family is not a new phenomenon, there are critical differences between the transnational family of the late 20th and early 21st centuries and earlier forms. Contemporary transnational families survive in a world in which communication and transportation technology makes it easier for them to stay connected. International telephone service, for example, enables families to talk to each other easily and cheaply, while video recordings capture family and community happenings so those living far away can participate vicariously. Airlines, trains, and buses make it possible for those with papers to make visits home.

The greater ease with which families maintain linkages is countered by the economic hardship and political and cultural marginalization of transnational migrants. As I noted in chapter one, many new migrants find employment in the low-wage service sector, work which is often temporary, part-time, and unstable. Their prospects are more limited than the prospects of migrants in earlier periods. Accompanying economic hardship are globally mediated images and messages of material wealth and American dreams, which conceal the harsh economic reality in which migrants must survive (Goldring, 1998; Hirsch, 2003; Mahler; 1995; Levitt, 2001). Therefore, the Hondurans in my research who have come to the United States since the civil wars broke out in Central America in the late 1970s and early 1980s, and who have continued to flee to the United States following the ensuing economic crises and the devastation of Hurricane Mitch in 1998, maintain their families in a radically different era of global capitalism than the immigrants of years past.

BRIDGING TRANSNATIONALISM AND FEMINIST CONSTRUCTIONS OF POOR FAMILIES

The study of the structure and survival strategies of poor Honduran families demands that we embed theories of family and carework in a transnational framework. As global economic processes penetrate deeper into family life, it is no longer viable to assume Honduran family proximity. White middle and upper class privilege and the access it has provided to the nuclear family have long been out of reach to poor families and especially families of color (Collins, 1994). Transnationalism pushes this analysis further by showing that not only is the nuclear family out of reach for poor families, but increasingly so too is the nationally based family.

It is also important to note the gendered structure of the transnational division of family labor. Men spend more time working for pay in the formal economy, and send home a larger portion of their earnings in remittances (Garza & Lowell, 2002), whereas women are almost wholly responsibly for family carework (Ho, 1999) and are more likely than men to be found working in the informal economy (Beneria, 1991).

The gendered patterns of transnational family labor hold true in other contexts of economic marginality. In poor communities throughout the world women are in charge of most household carework (Aranda, 2003; Cancian & Oliker, 2000; Mahler, 1998; Stewart, 1992). Women play an especially critical role as mothers, charged with insuring the health and well-being of their children and community (Chant, 1994; Dodson, 1998; Edin & Lein, 1996). Patricia Hill Collins (1994) termed the productive and reproductive labor which poor women do to ensure the survival of their children and community *motherwork*.

Poor women devise creative motherwork strategies to secure their families. For example, they often work more than one job, or piece together multiple part time assignments in order to make ends meet (Cranford, 1998). When there are no jobs, many seek employment in the informal economy, where wages are low, but few skills are required and work is flexible. Lourdes Beneria (1991) found that during the onset of the Mexican economic crisis in the 1980s, the majority of women managed to secure some income and that two-thirds of them earned it in the informal sector. A similar trend occurred throughout Latin America (Stewart, 1992). In the global north poor women also utilize the informal economy to secure wages, commonly doing outsourcing work in their homes or laboring in the informal service industry (Sassen, 1998). In both the north and south the informal economy is a haven for individuals, the majority of whom are women, who have been marginalized by processes of economic globalization.

In the global south motherwork increasingly mandates migration. Gender shifts in the demand for immigrant labor, specifically the increase in demand for paid domestic workers in the United States, Europe, and the Middle East has drawn mothers away from their children in search of survival wages (Hochschild, 2002; Hondagneu-Sotelo & Avila, 1997; Parreñas, 2001, 2005). They then send the wages they earn back to their families and communities who depend on them for sustenance (Chavez, 1998; Levitt, 2001; Mahler, 1995). Transnational mothers suffer emotionally, because they are unable to live up to their own expectations of direct care and nurturing (Hondagneu-Sotelo & Avila, 1997). In her study of transnational Puerto Rican families, Elizabeth Aranda (2003) concluded that the only sure way for transnational mothers to alleviate their emotional struggle is to return home, an option that is only open to those with economic resources and legal protection. Undocumented migrants rarely have the privilege of return.

Parents who have to work away from home, either for short or long durations, depend on alternative care networks to assist in raising their children (Aranda, 2003). *Other-mothers* are the grandmothers, sisters, aunts, daughters, neighbors, and friends who care for family and kin when blood-mothers are absent or unable (Collins, 1992). They are crucial pillars of poor families and communities (Collins, 1992; Dill, 1994; Dodson, 1998; Hondagneu-Sotelo & Avila, 1997). In kin-networks of other-mothers, *mothering* is defined by acts of nurturing and caring and not by a biological relationship of the mother to child. Stack & Burton (1994) defined kin-work as:

> ... the collective labor of family-centered networks across households and within them. It defines the work that families need to accomplish over time. The family life course is constructed and maintained through kin-work. Kin-work regenerates families, maintains lifetime continuities, sustains intergenerational responsibilities, and reinforces shared values. It encompasses, for example, all of the following: family labor for reproduction; intergenerational care of children and dependents;

economic survival, including wage and nonwage labor; family migration and migratory labor designated to send home remittances; and strategic support for networks of kin extending across regions, state lines, and nations (35).

Other-mothering is central in the history of poor communities throughout the world. Kin networks were critical to family survival in the antebellum U.S. south as slave mothers were prevented from directly caring for their children (Shaw, 1994). They also helped hold families together in the many decades following the end of slavery when African American mothers had to leave home to take jobs as live-in domestics, a move which often mandated migration from the south to the north (Stack, 1974). In Caribbean migration circuits, there is a long history of *child shifting* (See Gordon, 1987) from mother to grandmother as a response to economic circumstances (Plaza, 2000). Child shifting most commonly occurs when mothers migrate internationally in search of work, placing their children in the care of their own mothers. Because of the uncertainty of migration, children often remain in the homes of their grandmothers for long periods (Plaza, 2000). While child shifting is spurred by economic crisis, the direction of caretaking shifts from mother to grandmother has roots in the matrifocal nature of Caribbean families (Ho, 1999). While Caribbean notions of kinship suggest that whoever is most able should care for a child if the parents cannot, caretaking almost always falls on the shoulders of women (Ho, 1999; Smith, 1996).

In addition to insuring the health and physical well-being of children, other-mothers play a key role in maintaining family unity and easing the anxiety or emotional burdens born by children who are separated from their parents. This role is of vital importance in transnational families in which the blood-parent is absent for an uncertain, or prolonged period (Artico, 2003; Levitt, 2001). Transnational children face many challenges. Growing up in and between two cultures, and always being separated from one of them, they lack cultural fluency and comfort in either. This can trigger a host of emotional and behavioral problems (Levitt, 2001).

In a study of Latino families Ceres Artico (2003) found that caretakers can help ease this emotional strife. If, for example, other-mothers are consistent in presenting the absent parent as a dedicated mother and/or father who has made a great sacrifice for the family by going to the United States, the children are more likely to retain or create a positive image of them, and to be more at peace in their transnational life. Of course, this is not always possible, and intergenerational dissension is common (Artico,

2003). Bryceson & Vuorela (2002) used the term *relativizing* to characterize how individuals, both children and adults, maintain ties to certain family members, choosing to pursue some relationships while disengaging from others. This is commonly a strategic decisions which can lead to stronger family ties or to disbanding ties altogether.

Other-mother duties extend beyond close family and kin, to any community member who may be without, but in need of care. bell hooks (1984) asserted this form of community other-mothering is revolutionary because it subverts the idea of children and dependents as property, viewing them instead as a shared part of a community. In contexts of poverty, what is revolutionary is also practical. For transnational families, collective survival work makes the most logical sense, further challenging traditional ideologies of the nuclear family.

In accordance with black feminist theories of the family, the phenomenon of transnational families suggest yet another way that traditional notions of the family are class and race bound. When studies of the family are extended to transnational communities, new dimensions of the family and motherwork become apparent. We can see, for example, how kin-work extends across time and space. As such, this chapter contributes a transnational dimension to feminist theories of the family. It also draws attention to the economic caretaking contributions of transnational fathers, suggesting this as yet another form of motherwork, and a critical component of transnational family survival.

FAMILY STRUCTURE AND FINANCIAL FLOWS

Each participant in this study is the primary economic provider for at least one dependent in Honduras. The majority (twenty-five) of the participants in this study are providers for their biological children. All but one of these parents supporting a child or children in Honduras also supports at least one other family member there. Others in the sample have brought their children with them to the United States or they had their children while here, but still remain the primary economic providers for other dependents in Honduras.

The demographic and caretaking patterns of Honduran transnational families are distinctly gendered. Women in this sample have an average of 0.94 biological children in Honduras, and 2.44 biological children in the United States. For men the situation is almost the reverse. They have an average of 1.75 dependent biological children in Honduras, and only 0.4 biological children in the United States for whom they are the primary caretaker. In addition to children, many are the primary economic providers for parents, siblings, nieces, nephews, and in one situation, a godchild, in Honduras. Both women and men in this sample support an average of one and a half other dependents in Honduras.

The relatively high number of children that Honduran women have in the United States suggests the potential permanence of their stay here. Children born in the United States, even those born to undocumented parents, are citizens. All but five of the children in this sample who now reside in the United States were born in the United States. Parents I interviewed whose children were born here celebrate their child's citizenship as one of their most important accomplishments as parents, and plan to nurture the privilege that citizenship entails. This usually means not returning to Honduras, at least until their children are grown. The low number of children that men parent in the United States compared to the higher number of children they have in Honduras, may foster a stronger pull toward "home."

Parents cannot migrate if they do not have someone in Honduras to care for the children they leave behind. In my sample, grandmothers care for the majority of children in Honduras whose mothers are in the United States. Aunts and siblings care for the remaining. Birth mothers are the predominant caretakers for those whose fathers are in the United States. In the two situations in which a couple migrated together, the children who remain in Honduras are split between the homes of both grandmothers. There is only one child in this sample who is being cared for by his grandfather and this unique caretaking situation only came about after the death of his grandmother. There are no other children in this sample who are under the primary care of male family or kin in Honduras.

The structure of Honduran transnational families suggests that while both men and women are providing economic support for their families, women, on the whole, are doing much more of the direct carework for family and kin. Men's carework is almost wholly financial. The next sections detail the direct care and economic processes and actors involved in transnational care networks.

STRATEGIES OF TRANSNATIONAL CARE: KIN NETWORKS AND OTHER-MOTHERS

Other-mothers are essential for providing nurturance and care for the children and the elderly who are left behind. As noted above, grandmothers are at the core of transnational care networks, sometimes providing care for three generations of children. Doña Rosa, for example, is seventy-five years old, and lives on the outskirts of San Pedro Sula. Three of her children have migrated to the United States, and she has since raised five of her grandchildren. She told me that, "When Maria and Fidel got separated, Maria went to the States and left me with her three children, Dania, Ramirez, and Dañiel. I also raised Jenifer, Ignacia's daughter, as well as the daughter of my daughter Leticia. I had eleven children of my own and then I raised five of my grandchildren. But there was no other way."

Dorotea, who has been working in the United States for five years, would not have been able to leave without the help of her mother and mother-in-law who are raising three of her children. "Well, in Honduras my children live in two places. The littlest girl is Gina and then there is Dañiel. They are being raised by my mother-in-law. Karen, who is the oldest, grew up more with my mom. Thus, there is a division, two with my mother-in-law and one with my mom." Similarly, Diego and David, brothers who work in Chelsea, left their children in the care of their mom, Frances. After working twenty-three years in a banana factory and raising seven children of her own, she is now raising three grandchildren. She accepts the responsibility because the biological mothers are not around. David's wife has recently joined him in the United States, and Diego's first wife was killed. And so, Frances told me, "you do what you have to do."

Other female relatives may also take on this important caretaking role. Carla, whose sister is working in Boston, is raising her two children plus a niece, a nephew, and the son of her cousin. Carla calls herself the "mom in the meantime." She, like Doña Rosa, and the many other-mothers in this study, provides the direct mothering to her young niece, her nephew and cousin, while the parents who are working in the United States provide the children's financial support. Her motherwork extends beyond the basic tasks of feeding and clothing her nieces and nephews. She also guides them in their school decisions, demanding that they study English so that "they can compete for the good jobs," and she helps them understand why their parents had to leave. Because Carla has a good job for Honduran standards, she told me that she is able to be a "good" mentor and role model, making sure the children understand "how hard you have to work to make it," and that "you have to work even harder if you are a woman."

Mothers and other-mothers in Honduras commonly extend their motherwork beyond the household into the community. Magda, for example, takes care of her three-year old son and her two-month old baby while her husband works in Boston. She is also one of the organizers of a community cafeteria that offers free meals after church services on Sunday. The makeshift cafeteria feeds many hungry children and some families. Most of those they serve do not have access to support from family or kin in the United States. Magda sees her work in the community and church as part of her role as a mother and community member.

Doña Rosa also plays the important role of community other-mother hosting neighborhood meals weekly on the patio her sons recently built in the back of her house. During the weekly gatherings, Doña Rosa's grandson plays the guitar and different people lead the group in prayer. It is a festive yet serious ritual in which people celebrate the support they feel in the community, while praying that the future will be better and that they can keep going even though times are tough. Most of the people who come to the meals are alone, having been abandoned by family members in the United States. Doña Rosa feels that it is her obligation to share the money she receives from her daughters in the United States to help those who are less fortunate. Since the government does little to help the poor, she believes that individuals must do what they can.

> We are working on a project in the Catholic Church. . . . The Lord has called us for this work. Because we're not, not just there for fun, but rather the Lord has called us . . . to help in his work, visiting the sick people. Because the sick people have been abandoned, who don't have . . . their families, they are bad off. So the group, we spend time with the sick people, with the elderly, and there are a lot of elderly people. And what my kids give me, I share that, so the Lord blesses them as well.

Lourdes, who lives next door to Doña Rosa is the only one in her family who remains in Honduras. She never knew her dad, but she thinks he was an Italian who left Honduras soon after she was born. Her mom went to the United States when she was fifteen, leaving her in charge of her two younger brothers. Two years later Lourdes' brothers too set out to find work in the United States. By this time she was pregnant and unable to make the trip. Her mom and brothers sent money for a while to help her get by. But soon her brothers married and stopped sending money, and her mom's poor economic situation made it difficult for her to send more than $30 or $40 a month. Lourdes married. When her children were toddlers her husband left for the United States. He promised that he would find work, save money, and then bring them to the United States to join him. He never followed through on his promise. Instead, he divorced her, married an American woman and cut off all financial support.

Doña Rosa makes sure that Lourdes and her children have enough to eat, and that her son can afford the books necessary to go to school. She serves as a community social worker of sorts, a community other-mother to everyone in need. Doña Rosa understands, she told me, that the people's poverty is no fault of their own. There is no work in Honduras and "without family people have nothing."

Gloria also acts as a community other-mother. She lives in a small, comfortable, tidy house with her four sons. Her husband has been working in Chelsea for several years. While I was visiting with Gloria, two children from the neighborhood wandered into her house, and with a nod from Gloria opened the refrigerator to pull out a Coke and a snack. "They live down the street," she explained. "Their older sister takes care of them, but she has to work all the time, and so they often come here for a bit to eat, or just to visit. You know in Honduras, *mi casa es tu casa*, my house is your house. That's what we believe."

There is a shared sense among the mothers and other-mothers with whom I spoke in Honduras that responsibility to the community is an extension of family responsibility. Those who receive support from family in the United States feel lucky to have access to dollars in such dire economic times. And they know how tough life is for those who are not so lucky. In Honduras, families commonly share food, phones, and television viewing space with their neighbors. Community other-mothers make certain that everyone is taken care of, knowing that if something was to happen to them they too would rely on community other-mothers to take care of their own children and household.

I found a similar version of kin work and community other-mothering in Boston. I heard several stories of migrants who loaned hundreds of dollars to or shared housing with family or kin whom they barely know. There is a sense that it is a family responsibility to do what you can to help. Patricia, for example, has provided food, money, and shelter to three of her nephews when they first arrived in Boston.

> I had a nephew that stayed here with me for a time. I barely knew him, but he stayed with me for a while before going to North Carolina. Another time, another one came from Honduras. That was in 1998. And then there is the one now living below me. This one, well his mother died.... He looked me up, and I said okay, 'I don't have much, but in the basement there's a place to put a bed,' and he stays there.... Now I love him as if he were my son.

Many of the Hondurans I met in Boston spoke with pride about their commitment to helping family and kin. They were raised in close-knit neighborhoods where helping those in need was expected, a value that they complain is missing in America. In Honduras, I am told, and indeed I observed while I was there, few would close their doors to those who are hungry or without work.

The Strategies and Challenges of Transnational Care

Beatriz continues her other-mother practices in the United States. In addition to driving friends and family around to do errands and go to health appointments, she translates for those who do not speak English, and once a month she organizes a trip for the children of her family and kin who cannot afford to do "fun things." She is surprised by how weak community structures are in the United States.

> Back home we always cared for each other. And if I had to cook for a neighbor, when a neighbor was sick, I would go drop them food, or help wash her clothes or clean her house. I never minded because my mother always told me that when someone needs you just go, don't ask for nothing. If she gives you something fine, if she doesn't, don't worry about it. But then when I come here, I see everything different, you know. Like if I go to somebody's house to clean for her, she give me money. I am like, what is this? Don't do that. You see life different. At home we was always helping people, if they get sick you have to go care for them. Like that. Because over there, we treat everyone like a family. . . . I still follow the same. I know one day if I need it, they'll be there for me.

Transnational families depend on intricate networks of family and kin to do the emotional and economic carework necessary to keep them afloat. Transnational migration is rarely possible without the financial and caretaking support of kin-networks and other-mothers. While there are many families whose kin networks breakdown, those who stay intact are best able to negotiate the challenges implicit in poverty and transnationalism.

THE ECONOMY OF TRANSNATIONAL FAMILIES

> If you have family in the United States, and they are doing well there, if they have a good job, or are professionals or something, they send money to family here, who can then put their kids through school and lots of things. But if your family doesn't have a good job or anything, then you're probably in a bad economic situation here. . . . Because the main source of income here is having family in the United States that does well. And if they can get their papers and send for their kids, then everything goes well. That's the dream.
>
> —Nora, La Ceiba, Honduras

Financial remittances to countries in the global south have increased several-fold over the past twenty years (Garza & Lowell, 2002). Research shows that a clear majority of immigrants remit substantial amounts of money to their families and communities (DeSipio, 2000). A 1998 study by the Strategy Research Corporation found that immigrants who do remit sent an average of $221 monthly. This study also shows that men are more likely to remit money than women, that remittances go up as wages go up, and that as time spent in the United States increases, remittances decrease.

As the result of economic crisis and political instability, immigration to the United States from Latin America began to skyrocket in the 1980s. Remittances have since become a pillar of Latin American national and community development as well as family survival. As I note in the introduction, in many countries throughout Latin America, remittances are more important than exports to their gross national product (Garza & Lowell, 2002). On the family level, remittances contribute a survival subsidy of several thousand dollars a-year on average to poor households. Studies by Garza & Lowell (2002) concluded that immigrants who remit send between 6% and 16% of their income earned in the United States to their families.

According to the Atlas Survey (2003), remittances are Honduras' greatest inflow of foreign currency, comprising 15% of their gross domestic product. My respondents send an average of $242 to their families every month, which is slightly above the average cited by Garza & Lowell for Latino families. Economic variables may be a major factor in explaining the discrepancy. Wages in the northeast are higher than in many parts of the country while need in Honduras is likely greater than in other Latin American countries. That aside, Hondurans are remitting a significant portion of their wages to support their families back home.

Whereas both men and women in my sample send financial support to their families every two weeks or monthly, the amount of their support differs. Women send an average of $192/month to Honduras, and men send $292. This difference makes sense in that men are supporting twice as many children in Honduras than women. Because women have more children in the United States, they spend more of their income on family survival here. Another factor that may be at the root of the disparity is the wage levels of men and women. On a whole, as I show in chapter one, men are earning more than women, and thus have more surplus income to channel to Honduras.

In many Honduran families, remittances provide the only source of income and economic support. A Western Union branch stands at the center of all the Honduran towns and villages I visited, symbolizing the centrality of economic remittances to the lives of transnational families and communities.

The Strategies and Challenges of Transnational Care

Families use financial remittances to buy food and medicine, to pay school fees, make house repairs, and even to support informal businesses.

Doña Rosa told me that her life has changed dramatically since her daughters started sending monthly remittances.

> In Honduras it's almost impossible to have money in the bank even if you have a job. Even the work in the big *maquilas* only pays enough for you to live day to day. There's just not enough to live, for food, for electricity, daily things. And you have to pay transportation. It's all so expensive. . . . The money that I get from the United States helps me survive. Without it we would suffer more. We would live in a dirt house. . . . Before my daughter went to the United States, I was working every week, every day. I never rested. Now I go to work only Tuesday and Sunday. If they (my children) didn't help me I would have to work hard every day, even at my age.

Transnational migrants in the United States often bear the unenviable pressure of supporting family and kin no matter what their economic circumstance. The economic situations of many families are so dismal that missing even one remittance transfer can mean hunger and deprivation. Patricia comes from a very poor family. She told me that while she is fully committed to supporting her family, sometimes she finds it difficult to keep up with their needs, as her siblings in Honduras rely fully on the money she sends.

> My sister only earns maybe $15 a week, and that's not enough. So I send her $110 each month. . . . And sometimes when my sister asks for help, or someone else in my family needs help for their child, like last month when a nephew died, I have to send more money. For the funeral I sent about $400. When my other sister came to the United States, I had to give her $700 for the trip. And sometimes I just can't do it. It's hard. But you have to help by giving a little money so they can buy some clothes, buy some shoes. And for food, because now they don't even have money for food, and it's very tough.

Elena expressed similar concerns. In addition to supporting her children in Honduras, Elena is paying for the medicine and doctor care of her ill sister. Without the money she sends, the family would fall part and her sister might die. Elena feels stress and worry over her family's vulnerable existence. No matter how tough things are for her in the United States, she never fails to send money.

> My sister is sick, so I call her every Sunday, and I send money. The money is very important, too important, because if I stop sending money they won't know what to do. Every eight days I put in one hundred dollars. But this time they needed more for the funeral of an uncle that died, so I sent my whole check. They don't have extra for anything. They told me they didn't have enough money for the funeral and I didn't know what to do to help them. I couldn't sleep last night. I was tossing and turning thinking what I could do.

Julio says that his mother uses the money he sends to survive, and for nothing more. If he stopped sending money she would not be able to buy food. Because she is getting old, he worries that she will soon need more money to pay for medicine or doctor care. Luckily Julio has another brother who also sends money to his mom, which relieves some of the pressure. Still, it is difficult to keep up.

David is better off than most. He sends $400 a month to his wife and his mother. With this they are able to buy food, pay for the phone and the bills, and to "put a little bit away for emergencies." Having any sort of a safety net is uncommon among the poorest families in my sample. The few families who do have a surplus after paying for their basic needs commonly spend the money on home repairs or on commodities that increase their daily comfort. For these families, remittances help to live a more dignified and less stressful life. Nora, for example, uses the remittances she receives to pay for her basic needs, and also to make life more comfortable.

> My mom sends me money monthly, between $100 and $500. I always need the money.... Each week to buy food for a family ... you need at least a thousand *lempiras* ($100). The minimum wage just isn't enough. It's not enough for the food, electricity, or the transportation ... and then there is the gas and taxes and everything. And the electricity costs maybe four hundred or five hundred *lempiras*. So the money from the United States ... it's for our survival.... And our lives have improved a lot too, mostly economically. We have done well in a lot of things. For example, primarily the debts. We can pay them now. And we bought accessories for the house. It's all a little bit easier. We can better afford food, and things for the kitchen. And we have a television.

Life in Honduras is expensive, especially for families who want to "live like Americans" in terms of food, commodities, and entertainment. American consumer goods can strain a family's budget. Food costs are especially high if a family strays from the staple diet of rice, beans, and tortillas. Coca-cola, chips, and white bread are typical staples in transnational homes. And in every home I visited in Honduras, even in the poorest homes, there was a television and in most cases cable television. I was told that the $9/month cable payment was part of the basic family budget. Not only does television provide entertainment to the unemployed and underemployed, but it also is a means of connecting with family in the United States. Every night at 8pm, Nora and her cousins gather to watch a *telenovela*. When her mom calls at the end of the week to check in, they talk about how the story line is progressing. Telephone service is another expense that is part of most basic family budgets. Family members cite having a phone as critical to maintaining their connections with others. In many cases poor family members in Honduras even carry cell-phones so they can be reached anywhere.

Family members in Honduras say that they are better off, at least in the short run, because of the economic support and material comfort that remittances bring. Family survival in Honduras can be secured with a couple hundred dollars a month from the United States. With more support, a family can invest in improving their quality of life in ways that were previously unthinkable. My respondents celebrate tile floors in previously dirt homes, television sets, flush toilets, a refrigerator, or a car. Families that do not receive support from the United States are the poorest of the poor. Thus, the sacrifices that transnational migrants in the United States make in terms of their individual mobility are certainly not made in vain. Mobility may be an optimistic characterization of the path of transnational families, but the importance of achieving secure survival and increased comfort should not be underestimated.

In addition to the material and economic benefits that remittances allow, they also fund future migrations. Very few Hondurans are able to migrate to the United States without the financial help from family and kin. Beatriz described the way her family supports each other in their migration efforts.

> My aunt was the first one here. Then she brings her sister, then her brother. Each helps each other. Because we have a big family, and from each family they bring one child. Then I have one aunt in Honduras who has seven kids. She has one child here, and she's planning on bringing one of her sisters. And we always help. Like they helped me come, because my mother has four kids. And they helped my brother. They left two of my sisters. And now I bring one of my sisters. And the other one is staying over there with my mother. To get each person here, we all get together and everyone gives a little money until we have all the money we need, and then we send it.

Edith's family followed a similar migration pattern. Transnational family migration is an extremely expensive endeavor and would not be possible without a diversity of support.

> I arrived first. I worked to bring Pati here and helped my mom bring my other brother over, and then we all worked to bring my other brother over. My trip cost about $3500 dollars. My brother's trip cost $4000 and Pati's was $7000 because she got hurt on the way and she had to be attended to by doctors for almost two months.

In the United States, transnational migrants endure great sacrifice in order to accumulate a surplus to send to their families. They face the emotional burden of separation from their families and home country, as well as the economic and physical insecurity that comes from working in low paying jobs that have no benefits and terrible working conditions. My respondents told me of living in cramped, rundown apartments, and skimping on food and goods for themselves in order to have the necessary extra money to send home. Ignacia, a housing organizer in Boston who has a daughter and many other family members in Honduras explained,

> I've been stretching my dollars. I don't spend a lot of money. The school that my daughter attends in Honduras is very expensive . . . $200 a month. The money she needs depends, because she has to buy a lot of expensive books. Then it's more. I also want my family to invest something. I have a big family and that's where I spend a lot of money. I have twenty-three nephews, and ten brothers and sisters . . . I don't always help all of them every month, but if they are in need I lend or give them money. I have to. Imagine. Every one of them has two or three kids. They are struggling. They ask me for money when they are in need . . . If they are really needy, I'll send $500 or $1000. And I send lots of gifts.

Material and economic remittances are rooted in the values of motherwork. Most of my respondents feel it part of their responsibility as family members to give what they can to their families. Securing family survival is as important as securing individual survival. My respondents do not expect that their giving will ever be reciprocated at the same level. But they believe that sending what they can to family and sacrificing in order to keep family and kin well is the "right thing to do," and "the only way *para seguir adelante,* to move ahead."

Elena told me that because she makes such a low wage, her health is often threatened because of her responsibility to remit money every

The Strategies and Challenges of Transnational Care

month. Still, she could never tell her family "no." It would not be right. And so Elena endures "many difficulties, like not being able to pay the rent or . . . buy food for several weeks." Because she is undocumented and not eligible for food stamps, she often has "to go to certain places where they give away food." Diego said that his commitment to help his mom is the most important commitment in his life, and that he will find a way to help her no matter what. "I tell her that I'll always help her. No one has to tell me to do it. And no one is going to tell me not to help her. The day someone tells me to do that I'm going to tell them what they deserve to hear."

This strong commitment to family often means giving up the chance to save money or to live a dignified life in the United States. Ernesto, who supports his children and mother, told me, "I can't make money because everything I make is for them. Here I just keep enough to pay the bills and the rest goes there, especially for the kids." And Dañiela, a former *folklorico*, folk ballet, dancer in Honduras who now works in human services in Boston, said that she has suffered through abuse just so she could maintain her commitment to her daughter's future.

> I didn't have good clothes or a good jacket. The money that I had in my hand I sent to Honduras. I didn't speak English. I didn't have any confidence. I needed money for my daughter and for my house in Honduras. So I started working in the house of an American Jewish woman. It was horrible. She paid me $100/week. I worked five days. I had to clean the house. I had to do everything. I had to wash the plates. I had to wash the plates first before she'd let me put them in the dishwasher. And she didn't give me food. She only gave me the old food. I cried because she didn't give me anything. When she shut the door I robbed the food from the plates. It was hell. And the most difficult thing is that she made me scrub her dirty panties by hand (crying). But I knew that my daughter had to attend school. So I had to do it. I was in this house for one year, and I wasn't able to defend myself. It's painful to remember this. But my daughter is so important. For her I would do anything. The love I have for my child gave me strength. Everyday I was thinking how important it was that my daughter was able to graduate. And I knew that without my money she wouldn't have anything.

This example of sacrifice, although powerful, is not unique. I learned that transnational migrants in the United States are often selfless, in order that they can provide their families, and especially their children, with a shot at a "good life."

MAINTAINING EMOTIONAL TIES

Most transnational migrants arrive in the United States unsure about when they will be able to see their families again. They maintain their connections to family and kin by telephone calls and sometimes by letter writing. Among my respondents, weekly phone calls are the norm, though several families talk a few times a week and one respondent calls his mother and son every day. Phone calls are more frequent when a family member is sick, or if families are in the process of planning for another member to make the trip to the United States. They make the calls with phone cards, which are available in most convenience stores and restaurants in immigrant neighborhoods. Phone cards are a much cheaper option than paying for a regular long-distance carrier and they prove more feasible than managing a long-distance phone bill in a house in which five to ten unrelated people might live.

E-mail is not used by any of the families in my sample. Lack of access to computers for transnational migrants in the States and Honduras, coupled with illiteracy, makes email an impractical communication option. Illiteracy, or low levels of literacy, also limits letter-writing possibilities for some families. Francisca, for example, never learned to read and write. She told me the most difficult aspect of illiteracy is that it limits her ability to communicate with family and friends, and it makes her dependent on others.

The purpose of most phone conversations is to check in about daily occurrences and to maintain a basic feeling of connectedness. School, financial needs and health issues are typical conversation topics. Martin Angel talks to his wife and four sons two to three times a week.

> I always tell them to study. They play sports. . . . All of them play soccer. And to the oldest I tell him to do well in his studies, because it's okay to play soccer, but you have to study too. That's with the oldest who is fifteen. I think they are going to study hard. . . . Because I talked to them and they promise me that they will. My kids are always very good to me. They always say 'Papi, I love you a lot, Papi, we miss you, Papi, when are you coming home?' The baby doesn't understand, but the others know that the factory where I worked closed down, and there's no work in Honduras.

Parents in the United States expressed the greatest emotional distress about trying to maintain connections with children who were very young when they left. Young children have more difficulty understanding why their parent(s) had to leave, and they often do not remember the parent well. "When we talk on the phone," said Omar, the father of a five- year old daughter in Honduras, "sometimes she doesn't remember me. This is one of the most difficult things."

Finally, children frequently inquire about when their parent(s) is coming home, or when they will be able to go to the United States. Many told me that they answer this question untruthfully, but lovingly, with a version of "soon; we will be together soon." Others tell their children the truth, that it is too expensive or dangerous for them to make the journey. The truth tellers bear the burden of their children's disappointment and sadness. David still has not told his daughter that he does not know when he will be able to return. "She always asks me, 'How are you, Papi?' 'Here I am, daughter, working!' I say, 'Here I am resting and watching TV.' And she says, 'When are you coming?' And I say, 'Any day now I'm going to come to see you.'" Elena struggles to explain why she cannot bring her daughter to the United States. "I talk with my daughter on the phone every eight days. Every time we talk she says, 'Mami, I want to be with you. Why don't you take me with you?' She doesn't understand that you have to have a lot of money to come over. Right now it would cost about $6000 to bring her here." Paula too struggles. "My conversations with my son are very bad . . . difficult. He always tells me that he wants to come here, and then I have to tell him that he can't."

Visiting children is also a difficult proposition. Even those with the legal papers that allow them to travel rarely have enough money to visit their children on a regular basis, or to arrange for them to visit the United States. The respondents in my sample who can travel legally visited Honduras on average less than yearly. Sporadic visits, which most concur are better than no visits, present their own set of challenges. They can be confusing for children and painful for everyone upon departure. The visits put an added emotional burden on the mother, or other-mother residing with the children, as she is the one who has to explain the abnormal arrival and departure of the transnational parent. Mothers and/or other-mothers also described the difficult position of wanting and encouraging the children to bond with the visiting parent, while knowing that this bonding will make it all the more difficult when the parent leaves. Claribel, whose husband Diego is now a US resident working for a meat packing company in Massachusetts, explained the difficulty her children have relating to and making sense of their transnational father.

> The kids spend all their time with me . . . so sometimes I can tell they care more for me than him. He talks with them on the phone, but he only sees them once a year. When he comes it's difficult for them to

adapt to having him here. When he leaves it's sad, because they need to have him here. With time, you have to get them to understand that he has to leave, because his job is there, and here he can't do anything. . . . They even get sick when he leaves, because they get so attached to him when he's here. . . . But it's also very different when he's here. The atmosphere is different. Even they feel it. When he leaves, his absence is felt. They feel an emptiness. Because they are young, it will be that way until they understand how things are. . . . I have the job of making sure they are doing well, because I spend more time with them. They have gotten to the point of being scared of him, because he hasn't spent much time with them. I tell them they shouldn't be scared of their dad. I tell them that they should respect him but shouldn't be scared of him. When he comes to visit, they just keep looking at me. They say 'Mami, do I do what he says or not?'

Transnational migrants in the United States also suffer emotionally from being away from their families. Nagging, and sometimes debilitating sadness, loneliness, and depression are common among parents in my sample. Dorotea, who has two children in Honduras, one who lives with her mother and the other with her mother-in-law, expressed her pain in being away from her children.

> I hope that someday we will all be able to be together again. I have always said that I believe this is the biggest obstacle in my life, to not be with my kids. . . . Because when I was there with them I had goals, I studied, and I had enthusiasm. But here I have little enthusiasm. I'm always thinking about my children, what they are doing, that they are getting bigger, that things are happening in their lives, and these thoughts obstruct my ability to be happy.

The homesickness and loneliness that burden transnational mothers are often coupled with anxiety over their children's health and safety. When I entered Paula's apartment in Chelsea, I could immediately sense her depression. While her toddler screamed and kicked for attention, Paula sat stone-faced, sad, and overwhelmed by the difficulties of life. Her husband had just lost his job and she feared she would lose hers as well. But what is most difficult, she told me, is to know that her child at home may be suffering. Paula is so worried about her daughter's safety and well being in Honduras that she told her sister, who is caring for her there, "not to let her go out, not even to the neighbors." Although she trusts her sister, she panics at the thought of something happening to her little girl while she is away.

The Strategies and Challenges of Transnational Care

Transnational fathers like transnational mothers suffer the emotional hardship of separation from their children and partners. While mothers expressed sadness and talked of depression from being away from their families, fathers seemed even more overwhelmed by the loneliness of life without their wives and children. Through tears, Alfredo told me, "It's not easy. It is an emotional topic. When you come back from work you need a smile and a hug, and when you are alone life is harder, work is harder, because you get home late and go to your room and just see the four walls. There is no smile and no contact with anyone." Paulo too choked back tears as he spoke about how much he missed the direct contact with his family.

> It never leaves me, and sometimes the loneliness in the house causes me to break down. Apparently family in particular is what one misses, the relationship with your children, and the physical contact. Contact by telephone isn't the same as physical contact. You can be sure that sometimes loneliness does damage to immigrants in this country, because one feels so alone without family. Sometimes without support we do things that we don't want to do like turning to alcohol and drugs. Yes, it's for sure that loneliness really impacts immigrants. I miss my family so much; my kids, my relationship with my wife. I miss them so much.

Several male respondents spoke of excessive alcohol use and finding women on the streets as ways in which they numbed their loneliness upon arriving in the United States. Five of my seventeen male respondents in the United States now go to Alcoholics Anonymous every day. Two others mentioned alcohol abuse in describing male housemates or relatives. Alcoholics Anonymous, they told me, provides a pseudo-family structure from which they can find some support and nurturance.

The common struggles with depression, loneliness, and alcohol abuse among men may also be due to the downward mobility they have suffered in the migration process. The loss of family proximity is not compensated by an increase in status. Instead, the reverse happens. Men lose both family and status. Martin alluded to his decrease in status when he told me that one of the most difficult things to get used to in the United States is how independent the women are, and how they do not listen to him like they do at home. At "home," he said, "women stay in the house. . . . They are more traditional." Martin hopes that someday he can return home and marry a woman who will look up to him, "like they all used to do."

Indeed, upon their arrival in the United States, Honduran men's position on the social hierarchy falls below that of white women and white men

(Espiritu, 1997), and their patriarchal power in the household is often challenged if their wives take on paid work outside of the home, or if they had to leave their wives behind in Honduras. My data show that those who are in the United States without both their wives and their children seem lost without them, as they are their basic source of nurturance and masculinity. Thus they seek solace elsewhere.

While the women in my sample who came to the United States alone express sadness in being away from their children and families, they are also more optimistic about being in the United States and about their capacity to provide for their families. My data suggest several possible reasons for this. Some of my female respondents joined the paid labor force for the first time upon arriving in the United States and expressed a newfound sense of independence. While all the women in my sample have children in Honduras, eleven of the women I interviewed also gave birth to children in the United States. I infer from our conversations that the children that they have with them in the United States buffer the pain of being away from their other children. Finally, some women have better attitudes about being in the United States because their migration provided an escape from physical abuse. Three of the women I interviewed left abusive relationships when they came to the United States, and two of these women found a domestic violence shelter upon their arrival, which one said *"cambió todo,* changed everything."

DREAMS OF REUNIFICATION

Shared dreams of reunification help keep families strong and connected. Where the reunion will take place, whether in the United States or Honduras, is less important than the reunion itself. Dorotea said, "It's not the place I don't think. It's not the place; it's not that I like it here because it's here. If I had my children here then I would want to remain here. And if I were able to be in Honduras with my kids I believe I'd want to remain there. I believe that what's important is that I'm together with my kids and my husband."

Although my respondents do not care where the reunion takes place, they do recognize that even if they want to be in Honduras, the grim economic situation there makes it an unviable option. Parents are savvy about how limited their children's opportunities will be if they stay in Honduras, so if for practicality only, most want their children to move north. Paulo hopes for the day when he can legally bring his family to the United States. "If there is an amnesty I will bring them here! Here it is easier to move forward, much easier than at home. I love my family a lot, my children. And I have my parents alive, my mother and father. We talk twice a week, but really I want them with me." Paula told me that although she would ideally like to return to Honduras, she knows it is not possible, because the only way she can support her children is if she's here. Paula dreams of the day she can bring her children to join her in the United States. Then she believes, "life will be better," and "they will learn English."

Yet reunification of any sort is difficult to achieve. There are political, economic, and cultural barriers to families coming together. On the economic and political sides, one has to be documented and have enough money and assets to qualify as a sponsor for family reunification. The 1996 welfare reform legislation in the United States substantially increased the requirements for sponsorship, making it difficult for the poor to afford a legal reunion. Illegal reunification is a risky option which is only available if a family is able to access sufficient funds. Omar spoke in frustration about the challenges of getting his family together. "The plans for the children are really difficult. Sometimes I think about trying to bring them here illegally across the border, or to pay someone who could bring them across the border. But this would cost $6000 or more for each child. I can't afford this. Trying to bring them across the border would be our last resort."

Maria's sisters and brothers want desperately to join her in the United States. Not only then would they be together, they would have a better life, and a better future. When I asked Maria what she thought the possibility of achieving this would be she was pessimistic. "Although we're talking about it . . . well it's hard to come here now. Really, after 9/11 forget it. They aren't giving anybody papers to come over here. It's very hard. Still they all want to come to America. That's our dream."

Many of my respondents spoke emphatically about their commitment to bringing their children legally or not all. The dangers involved in crossing the border without papers are great, something learned by those who made the journey themselves. Edith's son wants desperately to come to the United States to be with her, but until he gets papers she will not allow it. "He wants to be with me and cries for me because he just has me. . . . But I don't know. It's difficult right now. Everything is complicated, because I don't want him to come like I did, without papers . . . Yet it's so difficult for a mother to be far from her kids. So I pray that when he is eighteen he will be able to come. That's our dream." Ernesto faces a similar challenge. "They want me to go there and they want to come here, but without papers it's very difficult. I hope that God will help get my papers so I can go there to bring them over."

Country and cultural differences can also pose a barrier to reunification, especially if a parent(s) has children in both Honduras and the United

States. Omar and Dorotea have one child who was born in the United States and is thus a citizen, and three children who they left behind in Honduras.

> We have a problem. If it would be possible, I'd like to bring my kids here. The problem is that my littlest girl was born here. So she is the only U.S. citizen. So we have a big problem that we don't know how to solve. It would be very difficult for my little girl from here to move to Honduras. Everything involved in this move would be difficult, the climate and culture and everything. It would be difficult for her. One day we want to have papers so that we can bring the others. But we are buying a house in Honduras because we don't know what will happen with our situation here.

CONCLUSION

Changes currently underway in the global economy are continuously altering family form and function. As such, the gendering of "survival circuits" (See Sassen, 2002), deserves more study. The recent shift, for example, in the demand for labor in the United States from manufacturing to low-wage services, especially the expansion of the care industry, has spurred an increase in female migration. This signifies a potential change in family care structures, as women, who historically migrated for reasons of family reunification, are now moving to seek work (Hochschild, 2002). I am concerned about who will take over childcare responsibilities in the home countries of the global south as fewer adult women are available to do so, and as grandmothers, who are the current other-mothers, have passed on. Changes in the gendered patterns of child shifting appear possible as men are increasingly the parents who stay behind.

The focus of this study on family survival strategies encourages further exploration of the durability of transnational family ties over the generations. Although there is no indication that the economic situation in Honduras will improve in the near future and therefore that family and community dependence on remittances will lessen, long-term transnational support is uncertain. The future survival of transnational family members in Honduras may depend on the financial loyalty of the second generation in the United States, a generation that has grown up away from their homeland. Will the second generation in the United States continue to support family members who are in many respects strangers?

Overall this data encourages scholars to hone in on the needs and survival strategies of the poorest families in the global economic system, many of whom are living transnational lives. Greater attention to this population would open up new spaces for dialogue between family scholars and scholars of migration and globalization, serving to deepen and broaden the literatures in terms of race, class, and nation, and grounding them in the realities of the most vulnerable who are all too often overlooked.

Chapter Three
A Week in the Life

Elena is typical of the Honduran women I met in Chelsea. She is forty-three years old, married, and a mother of six. Her two youngest children, ages twelve and sixteen, live in Honduras with her mother, while her four oldest children are now with her. Elena has been in the United States since 1992, and has not seen her youngest children since she left Honduras. She is undocumented and currently works in a factory packing cartons for $6.75 an hour. She struggles with depression; depression that she blames on exhaustion and the debilitating sadness of being away from her youngest children.

Elena's life follows a tiring schedule of factory work and carework. She wakes up every week day morning at 4:30 am. By 6am she has arrived at the temporary agency from which she leaves for her day's work assignment. She works from 8am to 4:30pm with a half hour break for lunch. She arrives home a few minutes before 6pm, and has dinner ready by 6:45pm. By 7:30pm her family has finished eating and she has cleaned the kitchen. By 8pm Elena is sound asleep. At 4:30am the alarm goes off again.

Saturday breaks Elena's weekly routine, as she doesn't have to report to "work." Still, there is plenty of other work to be done. She wakes at 8am and launches into a day of housework whose only interruption is a trip to Western Union to send $100 to her family in Honduras. Saturday night Elena looks after her grandson. He is a feisty, energetic two-year old. Although she tries to watch television while looking after him, it proves difficult. 8pm is bedtime. Sunday resembles Saturday with more housework, laundry, babysitting, and a few breaks for meals and television. Sunday night Elena tries to relax and prepare for the busy week ahead.

Paulo is also in his early forties. He is married and has three children. Unlike Elena, he has only been in the United States for four years, and he is alone. His children are in Honduras with his wife, and he lives in an apartment in Chelsea with four other Central Americans. Paulo works the night shift as a janitor for a large Boston university. Like Elena, he struggles with depression emanating from loneliness and frustration. He does not mind his work really, although he thinks he deserves a better salary and he would prefer working in the day. But he is tormented by homesickness. He relies on frequent phone calls home to sustain his strength and spirit.

Paulo's schedule runs opposite to the traditional nine to five workday. At 4pm he awakes and prepares to start his day. At 6pm he leaves the house en route to his daily AA meetings, which normally run from 7–9pm. From there he commutes one hour to work. Work begins at 10pm sharp and doesn't end until 6am. On most days Paulo is home by 7am, but there are days when he must stay and work until 11am. Although tired, he would never turn down the extra hours. When his night shift finally ends, Paulo is exhausted. After he arrives home, he showers, changes, and relaxes with food and television. Then it is time for bed. On regular workdays, Paulo is sleeping by 9am.

Weekends are a challenge, Paulo reported, for those who work the nightshift. On Fridays, Paulo tries not to sleep during the day so that he can enjoy the evening and sleep during the night. It is difficult, though, to switch sleep schedules, and so he tends to pass much of the weekend in his bed. Despite his tiredness, Paulo finds time to talk at length with his family, to wire money home, and to run any errands he might have. He spends most of his free time watching *futbol* on television or resting in his room. Paulo has few social connections; his main source of communication and support is his family thousands of miles away. He spends a lot of time alone, or in the company of strangers.

Limited resources, long commutes and work days and family responsibilities structure both Elena's and Paulo's daily lives. True rest is a rare commodity. Both of their realities are partially defined by their race and class. They are poor, undocumented, far from home, and working in low wage jobs to support themselves and their families. Elena and Paulo report struggling with depression, and they perpetually miss their children in Honduras.

Yet, in other important ways, Elena and Paulo have very different realities. Elena came to the United States to join her husband and was soon thereafter reunited with four of her six children. Paulo came to the United States alone and remains alone. Their daily lives reflect their roles within the transnational family. Paulo is the financial backbone of his family but is removed from all direct care and nurturing. Elena provides financial and direct care, although she too is separated from children. Whereas Elena

A Week in the Life

comes home from work and launches into her "second shift" (See Hochschild, 1989) of cooking, cleaning, and babysitting for her grandchild, Paulo comes home to strangers, watches *futbol*, eats, and tries to stave off the temptation to call home again. Frequent calls are too expensive for his budget.

Both Paulo and Elena send money to Honduras every one to two weeks, but while Paulo's caretaking responsibilities end there, Elena's take up almost all her free hours. Their struggles and responsibilities represent how the intersection of race, class, and gender structures the transnational migrant reality, and yet how important each of these individual elements is in shaping daily experience.

In some ways, the lives of transnational migrants are similar to the lives of middle and working class American parents. They are structured around the needs of their families in general and their children in particular. Transnational migrants do what they have to do to make ends meet and to secure whatever economic and emotional stability they can for their families. This often means working in jobs that have long or irregular hours, and/or working more than one job if full time work is not available. And like many Americans, they often struggle within their families over how to divide household and caretaking responsibilities, and how to maintain household tranquility.

In one very important respect the lives of transnational migrants' are very different than those of working Americans. Honduran migrants live in a transnational space in which great distance and political and physical borders separate them from loved ones. This reality colors almost every waking minute, as they must always be attuned to the needs of their families thousands of miles away. Parents who have had to leave children behind in Honduras told me that not a day goes by that homesickness and the yearning to be near the ones they love does not gnaw at them. My respondents reported that the most important time of their week is that which they spend on the phone reconnecting with children and family. Even if money is low and the cupboards are bare, my respondents always guard the money it takes to buy a phone card.

In this chapter I draw on data derived from thirty-four one-week time diaries to analyze the daily time usage of Honduran transnational migrants. Based on my data, I categorize time usage as follows: paid work (work done for a wage), carework (housework and direct care that one does for others), personal needs (bathing, eating, sleeping, getting dressed, going to the doctor, dentist, etc.), personal leisure (free time enjoyed alone or with friends), family leisure (free time that is spent with children who need care), educational activities (any type of educational class), organizational activities (any activities done with an organized group) and communication with Honduras (includes phone calls and letter writing).

Heeding inspiration from the time use studies Robinson and Godbey (1997) and Heymann (2000), and the work/family research of Juliet Schor (1992), and Arlie Hochschild (1989, 1997), I pay special attention to the gendered differences in time use. In large part, my findings resonate with the research they have done on working Americans. Honduran women are doing a disproportionate amount of the household and carework and enjoy fewer hours of leisure than Honduran men. But analyses based on gender alone do not paint an accurate picture of transnational migrant life. The transnational status of Honduran migrants, their poverty, and the survival strategies that ensue, also structure time use.

HOW DO TRANSMIGRANTS SPEND THEIR TIME?

Carework: Caretaking and Household Labor

Carework is at the center of most families' lives. No matter how limited one's economic resources, food must be prepared, children fed, the house cleaned, clothes washed, and the ill tended to. I conceptualize carework to include all the tasks undertaken to help care for and directly support family or kin. I include housework, cooking, shopping for the family, and all other work that directly supports the non-financial needs of the household. By contrast, I categorize cooking, shopping, or cleaning, for oneself, as time spent in personal needs. Carework does not include work done for pay to support family and kin.

Much research exists on carework in American families and more specifically on the gendered nature of that work. Arlie Hochschild (1989) presented findings on the dynamics of household labor where both the husband and wife were employed outside the home. From observation and in-depth interviews with fifty couples, Hochschild found that "working" women are taking the lead in what she terms the "second shift" of housework and childcare, and that this is causing tension in marriages. When men step into help with the second shift, tensions ease. Yet, even when men and women share domestic work, Hochschild found there to be less time to complete them, suggesting that time pressure had roots in the work place.

Hochschild (1997) confirmed the workplace to be the primary site for time stress, especially for women. Yet financial demands for many make a reduction in work hours unappealing, even if family friendly company policies allowed or encouraged it. Hochschild found that others are hesitant to decrease work time because in their jobs they find a sense of belonging and

A Week in the Life

self-esteem. In the latter case, she discovered that the tendency to work long hours is at least partly due to society's devaluation of childcare and domestic work. Across her sample, family and household consistently take a back seat to work. Hochschild's respondents assume paid work to be inflexible, and they take for granted domestic work and family hours as malleable. As such, they exerted very little resistance to the invasion of work into the family sphere.

Juliet Schor's (1992) research resonates with Hochschild's findings, showing that hours devoted to household labor have decreased as more women work longer hours outside of the home. Specifically, with each additional hour spent in paid labor, Schor determined that women's labor has decreased by one half hour. While there has been an overall rise in working hours for women, time spent in household labor and enjoying family leisure has diminished.

Jody Heymann (2000) in her study of working class and poor American families found that women's care responsibilities, specifically for their children, mean they frequently have to disrupt their paid work. Consequently, inequalities in the home, in which women are carrying more of the care burden, have a tremendous impact on inequalities in the work place. Until the unequal burden of care in the home is addressed, Heymann concluded, women will never achieve parity to men in the marketplace.

Robinson and Godbey's earlier 1997 study offers contrasting findings. They countered that since 1965 Americans have actually gained an hour of free time per day. Using minute-by-minute time diary documentation, Robinson and Godbey concluded that Americans greatly overestimate the time they spend working each week. Their diaries, for example, show that Americans have on average thirty-six hours of free time per week although they estimate to have only eighteen. Robinson and Godbey argued that while the total hours that Americans spend at work have increased because of women's exodus from the home and into paid labor, this has been more then offset by a cut in household work resulting from a decline in marriage rates and childbearing, and a trend towards earlier retirement. They also found that, while women do almost twice the housework as men, men are actually increasing their work in the home while women are decreasing theirs. In terms of childcare, Robinson and Godbey concluded that women still do eighty percent of the work, but because women are having fewer children, they are still gaining in free time. Thus, the trend is toward gender parity.

Similarly, Bianchi and Robinson (1998–1999) found that from 1965 to 1998, women's hours of childcare rose from 2.2–2.8 hours a day, whereas men's hours in childcare rose from .7–1.3. In terms of total hours spent with children, women's time rose from 5.3–5.5, and men's time increased from 2.8–3.8. Although women are still spending more time with children, men's carework has shown dramatic shifts upward, suggesting a trend towards more balanced caretaking roles between men and women, and more family time in general.

Honduran transnational migrants differ in many respects from the working Americans discussed by Schor, Hochshild, Heymann, and Robinson and Godbey. As I note in chapter one and expand on in chapter two, transnational families reported a split in their work and family responsibilities across borders and among several care providers. It is common, for example, that a grandmother cares for her three grandchildren in Honduras while her daughter in the United States works and cares for one of her children, either alone or with a partner. Married couples too are often separated between the United States and Honduras. It is therefore difficult to capture the transnational nature of the daily work family strategies these couples employ.

Despite these very important differences between my sample and the samples of Schor, Hochschild, Heymann, and Robinson and Godbey, there is one important similarity that resonates in our findings, and that is the gendered breakdown of work. Like "working" women in America, my data show that migrant women in the paid labor force carry a much heavier care load than men. There are many men in my sample who are fathers and husbands but who have lived far from their families for many years and are thus not involved in any direct family carework. To the contrary, all of the single mothers in my sample either bore children after they arrived in the United States or they took on the responsibility for other family members' children once they arrived. This puts them in the position of having to work to support children in both the United States and Honduras. Whereas some of the men in my sample fathered children after their arrival in the United States, none were solely responsible for them. These children either lived with the child's mother, or they lived apart from the child and mother, some providing financial support, but none doing any daily carework.

I learned that many men do not have the skills to do much of the family's carework without the support of a woman. The exceptions are those men who have lived for many years alone in the United States, and have thus learned out of necessity how to do domestic chores. Yet even these men say that while they will help out more around the house when/if they are reunited with their wives, they still view housework as women's work.

According to my time diary data Honduran women are doing a disproportionate amount of the housework and direct caretaking for their families. Excluding the childless male and female participants, on average

A Week in the Life

women are spending twenty-eight hours a week in carework, while men spend approximately five hours. There is no indication that they are moving towards gender parity in this area. Even among married couples in my sample, in which both are working in the paid labor force, women are doing much more of the carework/household work than men.

More evidence to support the women-dominated domain of carework can be drawn from my interviews where women frequently complained that they receive little or no help from their husbands in terms of household chores. Patricia, for example, is married and lives with her husband and three of her children in Chelsea. She works full time cleaning airplanes at Logan Airport and she manages the household.

> No one helps me in the house. My husband never does. My daughter, well she helps me when she wants to, but sometimes she is rebellious. I have a lot of problems with her. When she wants to help out, she cleans the house, washes clothes, everything, but when she doesn't want to, she won't even clean a spoon. That's most of the time. So I have most of the work to do myself.

Dañiela, like Patricia is married and lives with her husband. She and her husband both work full time, he as a janitor and cook and she as a daycare worker with Head Start. Dañiela has two children, a daughter who remained with her grandmother in Honduras and a son who she had with her husband after arriving in the States. Dañiela complained that she does all of the housework and that her husband holds tight to his *machista*, macho, attitudes.

> We both have jobs, but I do all the cooking and cleaning. He does pay most of the bills, but I do the work. He works two jobs, but he has his mornings free, so he will take my son to the bus.... But when it comes to housework, nothing.... My husband goes to play basketball with my son on the weekends, but I do the work in the home. He's a typical Honduran man in that way. He doesn't believe he should have to do any of the housework.

According to my data, marriage adds to the female carework burden. Single transnational migrant women do an average of 21.6 hours of carework per week, while their married counterparts average thirty-four hours. This is similar to both Schor and Hochschild's findings. Marriage means more work for women, but has the opposite effect for men. Married men who live with their spouses have lighter workloads than singles. While single men must fend for themselves in terms of cooking, doing laundry and keeping their rooms clean, married men are relieved of much of this responsibility. Only two of the five married men in my sample who live with their wives do more than ten hours of carework a week. Most of the carework they do is childcare done side by side with their wives. Taking children to the school bus or to daycare is another common way that married men help out.

Most men in my sample are married but are living apart from their spouses and children. Thus, as geography dictates, they do none of the direct family carework. The care burden of these transnational families falls on the shoulders of wives or other-mothers in Honduras who care for the children and the household while their husbands, sons, or brothers are in the United States. The carework that happens in Honduras, while invisible in the actual time diaries, subsidizes the lives of transnational migrants in the United States; if transnational migrants have children in Honduras, someone else is easing their carework load.

According to my time diary data, the carework demands of transnational migrants do not interfere with their daily paid labor. In the thirty-four diaries in this study, there are no examples of a woman or man leaving work to take care of a child or family member. This is contrary to Heymann's findings (2000), which show that work disruptions for caretaking responsibilities are commonplace, especially for women. A likely reason why my respondents are not disrupting their workdays is that the majority of them work in jobs in which interruptions are not an option. Factory work, commercial cleaning, and domestic work do not provide the flexibility for employees to leave the work site, even for a short stint, to attend to non-work matters. In most low-wage job situations, if an employee leaves, he or she may as well not come back. Two women in my sample spoke of trying to rearrange their work schedules so they could tend to a sick child or a child in trouble at school, only to be fired. Low wage workers are easily replaceable, which means poor workers who cannot afford to lose even a day's pay are forced to find alternative ways to tend to family care needs that arise during the work day. If an alternative caretaker cannot be found, the family member is left to fend for her/himself.

Paid Work

Juliet Schor (1992) argued that,

> The tendency of capitalism to expand work is often associated with a growth in joblessness. In recent years, as a majority have taken on an extra month of work, nearly one-fifth of all participants in the labor

force are unable to secure as many hours as they want or need to make ends meet. While many employees are subjected to mandatory overtime and are suffering from overwork, their co-workers are put on involuntary part-time (7).

This paradox holds in the case of transnational migrants. As Honduran transnational migrants are located almost wholly in the secondary sector of the U.S. economy, they tend to fall into the latter group in Schor's analysis, those who are put on involuntary part-time and/or are unable to secure the hours they need to make ends meet. Schor (1992) learned that, "the proportion of the labor force who cannot work as many hours as they would like has more than doubled in the last twenty years (1969–1989)" (39). At the same time, there are many low-wage workers in America who are working long hours by piecing together two, and sometimes more, part-time jobs. While part of my sample has been unable to secure anything other than part-time, temporary work, there are others who are working well-beyond forty hours a week. Yet, neither group is securing the income necessary to comfortably support themselves and their family.

The economic challenges that transnational migrants face include long hours, low-wages, and insecure employment. There are other obstacles as well. As Heymann (2000) suggested, low and middle-income families face more problems at home, in their neighborhoods, and at school, than do well to do families. The fewer resources a family has the more obstacles they are likely to face in establishing a stable and peaceful existence. Indeed, work hours and wages tell only part of the story of family well-being.

Not once in my observations and interviews did I hear a complaint about having too much work. Instead, the complaints were about wages, challenging schedules (like the night shift), and the instability of work. My respondents want to work. They have to work. Yet, because of economic constraints, no matter how many hours they put in, it is hard to build a family safety net.

Robinson and Godbey (1997) discovered that people tend to overestimate the time they spend working because they do not account for activities that occur that are not work related. For example, people may pay bills, read the newspaper or socialize during working hours. They also found that those who work long hours work less regular schedules and thus may have a distorted view of how much time they actually spend doing their job. Feelings of deprivation may also encourage the over-reporting of hours. This analysis does not prove relevant to transnational migrant employment. My respondents reported that they do not have the flexibility to do activities during their workday that are not work related. Just as transnational migrants do not have the privilege to disrupt their workday to tend to caretaking responsibilities, they do not have the privilege to take time out to read a newspaper.

Time spent in paid work, like in carework, is gendered. In general, men in my sample are working more hours in the formal economy than women. The men average fifty hours per week, the women thirty-eight. While both men and women work in temporary jobs, it is predominantly women whose work is part time. The women also tend to have more sporadic work schedules than men, like working eight hours one day and none the next.

Both men and the women spend significant time each day commuting. Commutes for women range from less than an hour a week to seventeen and a half hours a week, and for men from less than an hour to eighteen hours a week. The average weekly commute for women is four hours and for men almost six hours. Commutes are longest for those who work for temporary agencies. Temporary workers must commute first to the agency and then to their daily work assignments. Those with the longest commutes tend to live in the city, either Boston or Chelsea, but work in factories or agricultural sites one to two hours outside of the city. Because their work assignments are temporary, it does not make sense for them to move in order to be closer to their work sites. In addition, workers must live in close proximity to the temporary agencies that distribute their work assignments.

Leisure

Is leisure really leisure when it is involuntary? This question pertains to the majority of my respondents. It is particularly true for men who are here without their families. Most are struggling to work as much as possible to provide for themselves and their families. The agency of transnational migrants is restricted. In many cases the leisure they have is un-welcomed leisure, and in most cases limited resources and dangerous neighborhoods constrain leisure activities to watching television or spending time with families or friends inside the house. Migrants have little choice over where they work, where they live, with whom they live, and how they pass their time.

Men, especially those living separately from their families, have more leisure than women. Even though they are working more hours in paid labor, their low involvement in carework means they have more "free" time. Men typically work long hours, and then come home to eat and watch television. Sometimes they play soccer, or hang out on the streets of Chelsea.

The men in my sample reported less leisure time than the average American in Robinson and Godbey's study. This is due to their long hours of work, commutes, and their irregular work schedules. Several men work the nightshift, which they reported interferes with their leisure time and other daily rituals. Those who work the night shift spend much of their time off catching up on sleep instead of enjoying leisure.

My female respondents reported far fewer hours of individual leisure than my male respondents (Women = 7.75 hours, Men= 23.75). Most of the leisure women have is spent as family leisure with their children. Even when combining family and personal leisure, women's leisure times are low, below those of the working Americans in Robinson and Godbey's study. Transnational migrant women spend their limited leisure time watching *telenovelas*, going to the park (in the warm seasons), or visiting with family or friends. Only two women reported reading, going to a movie, or participating in cultural activities. As is true for men, women's limited economic resources coupled with their low education/literacy rates and their difficulty speaking and understanding English constrains their leisure options.

Educational and Organizational Activities

Going to school beyond high school is a privilege in the United States, as few post-secondary educational opportunities are free to the public. Scholarships and financial assistance for non-citizens, whether for university courses or English classes, are difficult to come by. Except for a small number of English as a second language programs, undocumented immigrants are excluded from financial aid. The undocumented in Massachusetts are not eligible for in-state tuition at state colleges and universities. It is perhaps for these reasons that only six of my thirty-four respondents are involved in any kind of educational activity. The majority of my respondents have limited financial and political capital, which translates into restricted educational opportunity. Three of the six are taking college classes and others are studying English. The six who are taking classes spend between three and seventeen and a half hours a week in the classroom.

All six of my respondents who are involved in some sort of education are women. All of them work in addition to going to school, and four of the six have childcare responsibilities in the United States. These women either have a husband or partner who lives with them and is willing to help out while they are at class, or they have the flexibility to go to class while their children are at school. And perhaps most importantly, all the women who are in school have been able to secure the resources necessary to pay for their educational activities.

Financial and human capital is critical to participation in education. The three who are taking college courses are doing so because they work in a human service job, which pays for their college credits. Also, all three have human capital in the form of English competency and either a General Education Degree from the United States or an equivalent degree from Honduras.

Although several men expressed interest in learning English, citing their language handicap as a primary barrier to their economic mobility, none in my sample are participating in educational activities. Childcare responsibilities, which are an obvious barrier for women who want to attend school, are not a barrier for most men. Time is also not a barrier, as most men report that they have more free time than women. Still, men typically reported spending their free time watching television, playing soccer, or socializing in the neighborhood center, and not pursuing their education goals.

In contrast to the limited participation of transnational migrants in educational activities, half of my respondents participate in some sort of an organizational activity on a weekly basis. Here, the gender balance is opposite that of educational activities, with ten men involved on a regular basis and only eight women. Four men and eight women are involved in church activities. Five men are involved in Alcoholics Anonymous, and two men and two women are involved in a community group.

Church is the most time-demanding organizational activity in my respondents' lives. Ten of the twelve churchgoers in my sample are members of protestant, evangelical, Spanish-speaking congregations. The other church devotee attends a catholic church. This uneven breakdown between Catholic and Protestant involvement may reflect the growing evangelical influence in Central America (Stoll, 1990). It can also be interpreted to mean that transnational migrants find comfort, support, and community in the evangelical church. Evangelical churches structure the lives of my participants more so than the Catholic churches. In my sample, Evangelical members spent from two to thirty-four hours a week in church activities, whereas the two Catholics spent between one and three hours a week attending mass.

In addition to providing spiritual support and counsel, my respondents reported that church, especially the evangelical church, gives them the strength to be far from home and to "make it through the hard times." Men cited church as helping them to stay faithful to their wives in Honduras, and keeping them away from alcohol. Women described church as a place of community and family strength. They enjoy many church activities because they can include their children and because the church is a space in the community where they feel immune to the violence of the streets.

A Week in the Life

Community group participation often overlaps with church involvement. Two women and two men in my sample are active in a Latino community group. The women see their community group and church commitments as serving the same purpose of building a supportive network of friends who share the same values and can offer support and encouragement. They also view church and community organizations as important means of building a strong educated Latino community. Many community group meetings and activities take place in Chelsea's Catholic Church. The Catholic Church frequently hosts educational forums on immigration policy and rallies to gather support for Immigrant Amnesty. The evangelical churches represented in this study are disconnected from community issues.

The two men in my sample who are active in a community group are motivated by their concerns about labor issues and inequality. They both spend between two and five hours a week volunteering as community organizers. Both the men and women who spend some of their free time every week participating in a community organization, also work in a community or social service organization. They appear more politically aware and involved than the majority of their peers.

Alcoholics Anonymous (AA) is the third and final organizational activity in which my participants are involved. Five men in my sample attend between two and seven AA meetings a week, which translate into between two and fourteen hours of structured organizational activity. There are no women in the sample who attend AA or who mention alcoholism as a personal concern. Alcoholism is yet another indicator of men's struggle with loneliness and loss of status and dignity in the United States. My respondents told me that drinking alcohol is seen as culturally more appropriate and acceptable among Latino men than women.

Finally, it is important to ask why only half of my respondents are involved in an organizational activity. Unlike educational activities, organizational activities are free. They also offer an easy way for transnational migrants to become part of a community, something that would seem appealing to those who suffer from homesickness and depression. I suspect that the reasons my participants have low involvement in organizational activities is multifaceted. Transnational migrants, especially the undocumented, may be fearful of any activity that would jeopardize their anonymity. As I detail in the next chapter, many transnational migrants, and more men than women, are isolationists. They have come to the United States to earn money to send to their families and to attempt to raise themselves up socially and economically. Unlike communities in Central America, which have a long history of organizing and reciprocity, transnational migrant communities in the United States are often fragmented, based on compctition for meager resources and not on a spirit of unity (Also see Mahler, 1995). In addition, when one envisions being in the United States temporarily, which holds true for men more than for women, investing time in one's community may not have much appeal.

Transnational Communication

My respondents reported that communicating with their families in Honduras is often the most cherished time in their week. While advances in communication technology, namely the advent of e-mail, have made long-distance communication easier for millions of Americans, Honduran transnational migrants continue to rely, without exception, on telephone calls and letters to keep in touch with their loved ones. As I detail in chapter two, high illiteracy rates paired with limited or no access to computers, constrain transnational migrants from joining the World Wide Web. Even telephone calls are no easy feat. As many migrants live in apartments with strangers, few apartment phones have long-distance service. Therefore, they must buy phone cards in order to place calls to Honduras, and many must make their calls from public pay phones. I learned that as inconvenient as calling can be, seldom a week goes by without at least one call home. Because many homes in Honduras do not have phones, especially in the countryside, families often have to arrange to go to a neighbor's house or to a public phone center to receive calls from the United States. Thus, calls are scheduled in advance.

Phone calls, and less often letters, are the only means by which long-distance parents can participate in the nurturing and raising of their children. My respondents use weekly phone calls to nourish their relationships with family and to demonstrate their dedication to their families' emotional well-being. They reported that they use calls to express their love, as well as to encourage children to do well in school, and to motivate spouses or other-mothers to stay strong while they are away. They also use phone calls to strategize visits and/or attempts at family reunification.

Women spend an average of 1.9 hours a week in communication with home, while men spend 2.5. The caretaking roles that structure transnational families influence communication patterns. Because men are in the United States alone, phone calls and letters home are their lifeline to family. By talking to their children once, twice, and sometimes three times a week, men can maintain some feeling of participation in their daily lives. While men provide nurturing to their wives and children during these calls, they also receive it. Calls home are a means of coping with homesickness, loneliness, and depression. The frequency of phone calls by Honduran men is symbolic of their desire to maintain the status and identity they had before migration. Phone calls are a means of keeping information flowing that promotes their standing within the community. The women in my sample also rely on phone calls to ease homesickness and to feel connected to those they left behind. Yet, because they are more likely to have family with them in the United States, they are not as dependent on their families in Honduras for emotional support. And because many women report being involved in activities or work that boosts their esteem and energy, they do not have to rely solely on calls from home to fuel their confidence and encourage a positive outlook.

Levels of free time also determine why transnational communication between men and women differs. Additional free time means more opportunities to call home, and more time to dwell on the feelings of longing for family in Honduras. Men in my sample told me that there are certain times during the week when they have to exercise maximum restraint so as to not make an unscheduled call.

CONCLUSION

Time diaries highlight the gender division of transnational family labor. All of the participants in this sample are responsible for the economic care of family, yet women are almost wholly responsible for the direct care of children and the elderly. For women, work and family do not have firm boundaries. Women work both inside and outside of the home, in productive and reproductive labor, to care for their families. Yet, there is a rigid division between work and family for men. They are separated by public and private, and by thousands of miles and national borders. That transnational migrant men in the U.S. are not involved in carework is possible only because of the unpaid carework that women are doing for them in Honduras.

Time use analyses suggest that men and women have different levels of connection with Honduras. That women tend to continue to grow their families in the United States implies a long-term or permanent stay and the possible lessening of their ties to Honduras. The investment that women make in education in the United States supports this thesis as well; they are literally investing in their U.S. future. Men on the other hand spend more time communicating with home and thinking about home. And they tend to live a more solitary existence in the United States. I learned that the men who are most involved in their host communities are those who are here with their wives or partners. In general, transnational migrants seem to invest in the place where the majority of their family and community live. While women maintain family in Honduras, the immediate demands presented by children and family in the United States take precedence.

Inequality structures daily life for transnational migrants. Commutes are longest and schedules most unpredictable for the workers who are most vulnerable. For many transnational migrants, leisure is involuntary. Even when leisure is both available and welcome, there are few activities that my respondents can afford to do. The ways in which their time use is structured is yet another illustration of their blocked opportunity in the United States and the ways in which global inequality and poverty impact the most basic patterns of daily life.

Chapter Four
Transamerican Dreams

> Dreaming, he could look to the north, to a sky of many colors billowing with white clouds. Somewhere up there- he knew because everybody said so- was a place of excitement and money. Breathing the sultry air on Calle Libre, he could not smell the air of Brooklyn, of Middleton Street in Williamsburg, with buses and an el, and streets so often cold and wet....
>
> From, *The Short Sweet Dream of Eduardo Gutierrez*,
> By Jimmy Breslin

The barrio of La Victoria is a typical working class barrio on the outskirts of San Pedro Sula. It is a mix of humble makeshift shacks and concrete two and three room dwellings. Its roads are wide, dry, and dusty, except for the dirty puddles of water which mark several enormous potholes. Chickens, dogs, and pigs wander freely, mingling comfortably with the barrios' human residents.

La Victoria is poor and jobs in the area are few. Whereas several young female residents work in the *maquilas* only a short bus-ride away, numerous families rely on remittances from the United States for their survival. It is easy to identify the households that receive remittances. Theirs are the houses surrounded by nicely painted concrete instead of wire fencing and they often have a car or pick-up truck parked out front. Some have newly built additions, and inside all of them, televisions, stereos, and kitchen appliances confirm the flow of U.S. dollars.

At the end of the main road stands the grandest of all the houses in La Victoria; a large, three-bedroom yellow stucco house surrounded by a wide concrete fence topped with glass shards for extra security. The house is rumored to be full of "luxurious things," including a large screen television, a stereo, and a dining room set. Its owner, David, has seen it only once. He is in the United States working to pay for the house and to support his family. His wife is now with him and his children live with his mother on the other side of town. And so his house sits empty. David is a hero in La Victoria. He has made it in America, his friends told me, and his house stands as a symbol of the riches America has to offer.

But in the United States, David's life is far different from the status he and his house command in La Victoria. He and his wife live with six others, two of them relatives and the others strangers, in a rundown apartment in Chelsea. David works fifty to sixty hours a week in a meat packing plant, cleaning and making sausages. The work is hard, but he has no serious complaints. Except for the cold that is; the plant is kept at thirty-three degrees which causes him to get sick frequently. After almost three years at the plant, David still does not earn a living wage and receives no benefits. Yet, he has come far from the $2/hr wage he received picking grapes in California when he first arrived in the United States. He told me that the work there was "the worst," "inhumane," but it was something he knew he had to do to get a foothold in his new country.

David has many dreams. He imagines a future of full time work, education, and prosperity for his children, and peace and comfort in his old age. He is ambitious and he is willing to do what it takes to get ahead. He works very hard and this he believes is insurance that someday his dreams will come true. Although life in the United States is more difficult than he ever imagined, that he bought a house in Honduras is already proof, he believes, that in the United States all your dreams are within reach. Like many Hondurans, David is a transamerican dreamer.

The United States has long been characterized in immigrant mythology as a nation of opportunity; a "land of milk and honey" where wealth and success are there for the taking as long as you are willing to put in the necessary effort (Chavez, 1998; Hochschild, 1995; Mahler, 1995). Accordingly, with hard work and the right values, everyone in America has the chance to pull her/himself up from the bootstraps. Throughout history, many immigrants have done just that; they have come to America, worked hard, and they have "made it" (Borjas, 1999; Mead, 1992). Yet, a changing national and global economy has made the situation much different for post 1965-immigrants (Portes & Zhou, 1993; Sassen, 1998). As I detail in chapter one, a diminished U.S. manufacturing sector, which historically provided job security and mobility opportunities for the working and middle classes, has given way to a polarized service sector in which low-skilled and unskilled workers are often concentrated in temporary, poverty-wage jobs (Portes & Zhou, 1993). Many of the jobs that do remain in manufacturing are dangerous and low-paid. The missing middle of the U.S. economy means that the mobility opportunities for poor and unskilled migrants have been greatly reduced. But have their dreams been reduced as well, or is the American dream still a core part of the transnational imagination?

In this chapter I analyze the aspirations of Honduran transnational migrants and their relationship to the American dream. I argue that despite the structural limitations that Honduran transnational migrants face in the United States, most continue to believe that the dream is within reach. My respondents are rugged individualists, loyal to family but few others, and they believe passionately that hard work brings success. I find that they reproduce this ideology and that of American consumerism transnationally by sending messages, some true and some false, of success and opportunity to family and kin back home. And so, although most are neither citizens nor residents, they are important participants in the maintenance, reproduction, and export of U.S. cultural ideologies. Finally, I argue that living in a transnational space makes the dream more viable for transnational migrants than for other poor Americans. In this case, the American dream is truly a transamerican dream.

TRANSMIGRATION, SOLIDARITY, AND THE AMERICAN DREAM

Sarah Mahler (1995), in her major ethnographic study of Central and South Americans on Long Island, New York, found that they were on the whole dissatisfied with life in the United States. They told of arriving in the United States surprised to find the ugly reality of long and strenuous hours of work and an unwelcoming community. Even after years of hard work, her respondents reported that they still had not found the "success" they dreamed about and many said that if they had known how difficult life was going to be in the United States, perhaps they would not have come. Yet, despite their failures and frustration, they said that they continue to embrace the cultural ideology of the American dream. They believe they are the authors of their own fate, and with their arrival in the United States they have become "evermore committed to effort as the key to success" (228).

Their analyses of immigrant hardship do not include the structural barriers, including low wages, discrimination, and occupational and residential segregation, that greatly impact their existence. Instead, Mahler's respondents view their failed efforts at success as their own doing or as the fault of other deviant minorities. Mahler concluded that immigrants firmly believe that those who are poor and marginalized in the United States are so because of their own laziness.

Mahler argued that the competition between migrants has roots in their transnational responsibilities. They feel intense pressure to earn a surplus in order to remit money and goods to their families. Because the mainstream economy does not offer them jobs that pay a living wage, poor migrants find that they can often do best by supplementing their low wages with informal work in their own community. Informal work opportunities arise out of the many service gaps which exist in poor neighborhoods. Migrants with extra resources can exploit these gaps to make extra money. For example, they may rent out a spare room in their apartment or use their cars as pirate taxis, often charging above market prices to their captive audience. Following this strategy, migrants tend to stay rooted in their own communities, except when commuting to jobs in the formal sector.

My research resonates with many of Mahler's findings. My respondents too are individualists who hold firmly to the basic tenets of the American dream, while disowning much of the ethnic and community solidarity that they told me characterized their lives in Honduras. They told me that they continue to be surprised by how tough life is in the United States. They complained about discrimination in the work place, dangerous, treacherous work conditions, low pay, poor housing, and the injustice of paying taxes without being granted residency. Yet, few cited these as barriers to their mobility. My respondents are working hard (an average of fifty hours per week), yet as chapter one details, few are experiencing upward economic mobility and many feel tremendous insecurity in their daily lives. Still, they believe that they can and will achieve their goals if they continue to work hard and to sacrifice, and they look down on their peers and on native-born minorities who they feel do not embrace the same values.

Julio is twenty years old. He came to the United States after his family's small plot of farmland was badly damaged by Hurricane Mitch. Young and strong, he said that it only made sense for him to follow his brother's lead by making the trek north in search of work. He crossed the border at age fifteen, spent six months in immigration prison in Texas, and then came to Chelsea, where he has worked since his arrival. His life in the United States has been characterized by hardship. Poverty wages, lack of job security, and discrimination have been his experience. But when I asked him about his goals and about the opportunities that he thinks are available for Hondurans in the United States, he espoused the optimistic belief that in the United States you can do anything if you put your mind to it. "There aren't any obstacles here. Everything you want to do can be done. That's what I think. God will help us come out ahead."

Elgardo works the night shift as a janitor in a Boston office complex. He has suffered injuries and mistreatment on the job, and because he has no health coverage his injuries have gone untreated. Like Julio he is undocumented, which limits his ability to protest his bad work conditions. At one point he complained to his supervisor about the job's persistent hazards, but he was told that if he did not like the job he could leave; a move that he does not have the privilege to make.

> I work as a janitor . . . and our supervisors treat us really badly just because we are immigrants. Some of my supervisors are Hispanics and they should know not to treat us this way, but they do. . . . We work with dangerous soaps and liquids that make you sick. I have burned my hand with the chemicals but they just put me back in the same job. But the worst is that when I asked my supervisors for help paying to go to the doctor he told me they couldn't help. I went to the clinic anyway but they said I needed a letter from my boss and he wouldn't give me one. . . . The truth is that when one arrives at this job they say that it is easy and they don't tell you what the conditions are like. And they don't tell you that you will have to work nine hours but they will only pay you for eight. They can do this because they know that the majority of us don't have good papers.

Elgardo does not enjoy even basic workers' rights. He has dedicated himself to the commercial cleaning company that employs him, but there is no indication that he will move up in the company or that he will ever earn a "decent" salary. Elgardo wishes that the United States government would give immigrants more credit for their work, but on the whole he does not blame U.S. society for his woes. Despite his hardship, he wants to stay in the United States and continue to work, because it is only in the United States, he told me, that he can reach his dreams.

> I want to stay here, because if you work here you can obtain the level of life that you want. For this I like this country. If you like to work hard you can get what you want. Of course it's not fair that the government knows we pay taxes and do the jobs that Americans won't do, but we still don't get papers. . . . But I understand that I can't occupy a better position without the skills. . . . I understand that I am where I am for a reason. . . . And here the opportunities are better. I like this country.

My respondents take pride in their histories of struggle, of fighting for what they want, and of sacrificing. Dañiela, who faced severe mistreatment during her experience working as a live in housekeeper for a wealthy family in New York told me with tears in her eyes, "I have struggled, I have been hungry.... But I'm here. I'm here and I can do it.... You have to fight for your dreams. You have to fight." And Ramon, who has endured persistent lay-offs and pay cuts, expressed what seemed to be a peaceful acceptance of the inequality and suffering immigrants face and the sacrifices they must make. According to Ramon, "... it is just the way it is, and if you are strong you will make it anyway. You come to reach a goal, and you have to put up with pain in life, if you really want something. It is a sacrifice. And things have a cost, because it's always going to be that some have more and some have less. I think that it is always going to be like that."

Ignacia, a housing organizer in Boston seconded Dañiela's and Ramon's advocacy of struggle and sacrifice. A self-identified fighter for the poor and disenfranchised, she believes that what the poor need most is the "courage" and "drive" to take the risks necessary to make it in America. Even though she has enjoyed unique supports to which most immigrants have not had access, such as receiving her papers under the 1986 amnesty, a Section Eight housing subsidy, and social work support in getting her General Education Degree and her first job in human services, Ignacia attributed her self-identified "success" to hard work and ambition and she criticized those who have not been as successful for not demonstrating the same drive. "I think that you have to have courage, strength. You have to persist. You have to have a mission. You have to have ambition. And that's what a lot of people don't have. They give up. People give up. You know, I see it, because I see some close friends who have been here for many years, and they haven't gone anywhere."

Like Ignacia, Veronica expressed her belief that she has "made it" in America. Although she came to the United States without papers, she is now married to an American and has a green card. She too has had unique supports. She is from a middle class family and arrived in the United States on a tourist visa, a tell-tale symbol of status within the community of undocumented Hondurans, she arrived with some resources, and she had an aunt and uncle who supported her until she was able to get on her feet. Veronica's family in Honduras owns a large farm whose success she attributes to her father's hard work. She is grateful to her father for passing his work ethic on to her and for teaching her to always have a goal. She believes her work ethic and her goals have gotten her to where she is now. Veronica is sad and surprised by the lack of values displayed by other Hondurans. In our interview, she asserted that it is a result of their weak value system that they remain poor.

> I'm disconnected with my community. When I'm at work and I hear someone from Honduras I will try to help, but I know they have their own social life in different ways. I don't get together with them. Number one, they drink a lot. I don't know where they are coming from,

what city or what part of Honduras, but they're not thinking, and they're not ambitious people. . . . I'm not connected because I choose not to be. . . . Plus they just work. They don't go to school. Can you imagine? It's sad, very sad. . . . I don't know why it is. When I came over here and saw all the facilities, that I could work in the day and go to school at night, I was in heaven. I knew I was going to do it.

Ironically, the cultural ideology embraced by the majority of my respondents is more closely aligned with political and economic conservatives than with the liberals and radicals who historically have been their advocates. Because they hold firmly to their belief in individual agency as the key to upward mobility, Honduran transnational migrants do not tend to support policies that challenge the status quo. My respondents are overwhelmingly anti-government in general and anti-welfare in particular. They believe that to make it in America they have to do it on their own, and they criticize other minority groups for exploiting the U.S. government's social and economic assistance.

Only two of my thirty-four U.S. respondents have accessed government assistance of any sort, and most pride themselves on never having gotten help. This is true of Francisca, an elderly woman who received her residency in the eighties and thus qualified for public assistance. She has worked most of her life, beginning at the age of eight when she began helping her parents in the fields of northern Honduras, and she has raised ten children on her own. Even when pressured by her son to apply for public assistance, she refused. "I've never gotten help from the government. No, no, no. Until now, the only help I got was some free care at the community clinic, but government help, no. I've never liked it."

The two respondents who did get assistance defended their use of welfare as an emergency measure, which they used only a short while until they could get back on their feet. Both of them applied for assistance after leaving abusive relationships and while pregnant, and they were guided through the process by social workers at a shelter. If left to their own devices I do not think they would have sought government help. Although the majority of my respondents have never been eligible for assistance, it remains relevant that they curse it as unnecessary and debilitating for those who use it. All they want, they told me, is the opportunity to work.

MAKING SENSE OF THE STRUCTURAL/IDEOLOGY MISMATCH

My interview data reveal what seem to be deep contradictions between the daily reality of migrants and their ideological commitments to the American dream. Their lengthy narratives about being in America and managing daily life are complex and conflicting. In interview after interview my respondents shared stories about discrimination in the workplace, inequality in wages, as well as unfair and abusive treatment by employers. They reported poor working conditions and long and arduous workdays. And accompanying these descriptions was an overtly political analysis, with interviewees commonly using words such as "exploitation," "unjust treatment," "fear provoking," and even "fascist," to describe employers and work experiences.

Yet when I asked them if they felt there were barriers to socioeconomic mobility in the United States, only a few answered in the affirmative. The majority smiled and said something to the tune of, "No, this is a land of opportunities." Even when I prodded my respondents about this paradox, the discussion did not seem to unravel the contradiction. Baffled, I presented the material in an interpretive focus group that included Honduran transnational migrants, Honduran service providers, and community organizers. Anita, a lay pastor in the Boston area spoke first.

> The reality is, where we come from is really poor. There are no opportunities. None. Even if you want to work hard, there are no jobs. Here it's hard, but we have no choice but to accept it. But we know that Americans don't understand our reality. So we don't offer to talk about it too much. It's better and safer to talk about the hope that we know we should have. And really, we do have hope. We have to have hope.

Focus group participants also spoke about how difficult yet important it is to gain respect from native-born Americans. Participants feel passionately that they deserved Americans' respect, but that they seldom receive it. The only way to earn it is to prove themselves as hard workers who value the sacrifice and commitment it takes to make it in America. In addition, migrants will not let Americans know if they are suffering. As Rosalia said, "No one is going to tell you, an American, that there are problems with your country. They may say that their work situations are difficult or that certain individuals are cruel, but they won't attack the system. They would be afraid of looking anti-American and weak."

Another participant asserted that respect aside, to talk to an American at all is a risk, even if she/he is a trusted friend of the community. The climate of fear following September 11 has increased the barriers between migrants, especially the undocumented, and native-born Americans. Isabel reminded me, "Even though you are a friend in this community, you're a gringa, and there's fear. People are being deported around here; there are people being deported right now as we're talking. It's scary to speak critically of America to an American even if we're told that they are 'safe.'"

The interpretive focus group data also reveal just how intensely the poverty of Honduras impacts how transnational migrants make sense of their opportunities in the United States. From the perspective of many of my respondents they are succeeding because they are surviving, and even more, they are affording opportunities and material goods that they and their families never could have dreamed of before they came to the United States. The focus group data also show that hope is all the more powerful when it is the only thing to hold on to. This is something that migrants do not imagine native-born Americans can understand.

MAKING THE DREAM VIABLE

While I argue in chapter one that upward mobility in jobs and income are rare among poor Honduran transnational families, financial remittances enable poor families in Honduras to purchase material goods and to make their lives more comfortable. My respondents reported buying new household appliances, televisions, cell phones, cars, and in some situations, a home. This asset accumulation and the boost in status transnational families enjoy because of their newly acquired material goods can be interpreted as a form of mobility (Goldring, 1998; Levitt, 2001; Mahler, 1995). These assets carry a lot of weight in the transnational migrant imagination. Assets, like David's house and his neighbors' new trucks and appliances, symbolize success. All of this is not to suggest that American dream advocates have been correct all along. Instead, it is to say that the American dream appears more plausible when it is interpreted in a transnational context.

The disparity between the United States and Honduras in terms of average income and cost of living paradoxically makes the American dream more attainable. My respondents construct and seek their goals in a transnational space, and when the poverty wages they are earning do not allow them to fulfill a material dream in the United States, they can try to fulfill it in Honduras. Because they maintain strong transnational ties, their physical presence is not necessary for the logistics of their plan to be carried out. For example, several of my respondents spoke of building or buying a home in Honduras even if they did not know when or if they would ever return. Others spoke of the goal of someday opening a business in Honduras. My respondents reported feeling like they are "here and there." They want and need the income they earn in the United States, but their hearts remain in Honduras, and they yearn to fulfill their dreams and enjoy success with their family and community.

Dorotea is a transamerican dreamer. She lives with her husband in a run-down apartment in Massachusetts. They have always dreamed of owning a new house. When they were planning their journey to the United States they believed that they would be able to someday buy a house here, but they soon realized that their slim wages coupled with their undocumented status would make this nearly impossible. Still, they persisted. They decided that instead of using their meager surplus earnings to move to a better apartment in the United States, they would send all of their extra money to Honduras where they could better afford to invest in the kind of life they really want. Although they have no plans to return to Honduras in the near future, they put a $500 down payment on a house on the outskirts of Tegucigalpa. Three of their children remain in Honduras and Dorotea hopes that some day they will all live together in *"la casita de nuestros sueños,* the house of our dreams."

> The house we bought is in a very pretty colony in the city . . . It is a big house and it is new. Nobody has ever lived in it. And it was just built. My sister took care of all the paperwork we needed to do to buy it. It has a large patio, just like we always have wanted. It has two bedrooms, a kitchen, a living room, and a bathroom. My sister says it is beautiful. We never saw photos of the house before we bought it, and we still haven't seen any, but my sister sent us a record from the newspaper talking about the new colony, and Omar and I both knew it was what we wanted. We are making a huge sacrifice to pay for it, but it is worth it.

Dorotea and her husband sacrifice comfort in the United States in order to channel their surplus earnings toward the goal of someday living comfortably in Honduras. They do not know when they will be able to return to Honduras, but they told me they feel happy and proud that they have fulfilled their goal of home ownership, and they maintain the hope that someday their family will be together.

Francisca too uses all of her extra savings and resources to fix up and pay for her house in Honduras. Her house is both a material goal and a safety net for old age. Already in her seventies, she knows there will be a day soon when she will be unable to continue working in the United States. Because she has been working in the informal sector, she will not be able to collect any social security. So, she will return to Honduras to live in the house that she owns, within a community of friends and family who will take care of her. "When I can't make it any more, when I can't support myself, I'm going . . . to my country. That's why I'm killing myself to get my house all fixed up. So when I die, I have my little house."

A house also provides a sense of security. While the majority of my respondents reported that they want to stay in the United States for as long as possible, those without papers know that deportation is a real risk. Even those who have papers fear a time when there will be no more work and they will have to return to Honduras. For still others, a house in Honduras would provide them the chance to move back and forth. While economic necessity tends to dictate the decision to stay in the United States, all of my respondents want to at least someday be able to visit Honduras on a regular basis.

> When you leave your country, you come with goals, but sometimes it's very difficult. I haven't bought a house in Honduras. . . . I am thinking of buying one in the next two years in Tegucigalpa, the capital. I don't necessarily want to go back there, but I want to buy a house. When you go there, you want to have a place to stay, right? Also, you don't know what's going to happen in the future, you can always change your mind. Because maybe someday I would like to go and live there. It's an idea, but you never know.

Sixteen of my respondents own homes in Honduras. Eight others said they aspired to buy a house. Of the sixteen homes that my respondents own, eight are being occupied by their family or kin. The other eight sit empty. Francisca, Veronica, Beatriz, and Marta built or bought their homes with the plan of living there after their "retirement" in the United States. The others are uncertain when or if they will be able to return to occupy their homes.

In addition to dreams of home ownership, my respondents spoke of using the transnational space in which they live to pursue their dreams of entrepreneurship. David has already achieved his dream of home ownership, and now dreams of "giving back" to Honduras by starting a business there. He imagines that by continuing to work and develop connections in the United States he will someday have the funds and support to start a company in Honduras. The business would provide him the opportunity to be both "here and there." His dream is large, but he thinks it will be possible to achieve.

> Well it's not that I really want to stay, but I would like to have a good economic situation, stability, socially, and everything else so I have to stay. . . . If I could I would stay six months here and six months in my country. I would like to give back to my country as well! Not just this country. I've seen on television how the Mexicans have companies in their country, so that's what I'd like to do . . . to give work to the people. . . . Sometimes I think I would like to have a banana company.

> Make some money and have economic support from here. Because you can find someone, companies that support you economically. I mean, say I had the land, and they would administrate the other things I need, fertilizer, machines, everything I need, packing materials, everything. So then we would be partners. That's how I want to work.

Beatriz too wants to start a business in Honduras. Like David, she envisions splitting her time between the United States and Honduras.

> I plan to stay here until the kids grow up and go to college . . . and then I want to leave and do my own business over there, and just come here every three months to see my kids. When they can depend on themselves, I'll be free myself. And then I'd go back. I want a hair salon or maybe a grocery store, because they don't have one. Well, they do have it, but I want to put one where I live . . . because over there they don't have a grocery store. . . . So I was talking the other day with my friend. And he said , 'Why don't you start a grocery store back home Beatriz? Cause you always are doing things with business. I said, 'that's a good idea.' So now I'm going to do it.

Paulo has business dreams as well. His idea is "to save money and then return to my country and start a business with my wife. I've always wanted my own business."

In a couple of cases entrepreneurial plans are already in play. Martin Angel, for example, has helped his wife set up a small storefront in their home. Martin Angel's four sons work at the store before and after school and his wife tends it the rest of the time. They began by selling only candies and sodas, but now they stock grain, rice, and basic household supplies. Almost all the money Martin Angel sends every month goes into the store. It is Martin Angel's dream that some day the store will be profitable enough for him to be able to return to Honduras.

In another case, Ignacia helped her mom set up an informal business selling lingerie. Ignacia sends discount lingerie to her mom from the United States who then sells it in town. The profits from the business are such that Ignacia's mother will soon be able to retire, a privilege she never dreamed about before Ignacia migrated north and started remitting money and ideas.

TRANSAMERICAN DREAMS AND CONSUMER SOCIETY

Scholars have observed that the American dream has been altered over the last few decades by an increase in conspicuous consumption (Cohen, 2003;

Frank, 1999; Schor, 1998). The goal of simple home ownership has been inflated to that of mansions and penthouse suites, and the middle class symbol of the family station wagon has been replaced by the sports utility vehicle. Success is no longer defined by comfort and security, but by financial wealth and material excess. Robert Frank (1999) claimed that Americans have "luxury fever." Similarly, Lizabeth Cohen (2003) suggested that consumption is at the root of the United States' evolution into a "consumer's republic," and a changed American experience in which consumption is linked to wealth and prosperity. While this new American dream is sold to the masses indiscriminate of class or income, few can afford its inflated price tag. At the same time that celebrations of affluence and materialism abound, inequality in America continues to intensify (Frank, 1999; Schor, 1998).

The globalization of media, especially media's reach into the poorest regions of the global south, has further accentuated the distance between the "real" lives of consumers and those portrayed on screen and in print. Arjun Appadurai (1996) used the term *mediascapes* to describe both the technology through which information is disseminated globally and the images created by global media. He suggested that through mediascapes, news, entertainment, and advertising blend. It is through mediascapes that many people who live far from the centers of global power develop their understanding of what life in the centers is like. For consumer audiences in the margins of the global economy, "the lines between the realistic and fictional landscapes they see are blurred, so that the farther away these audiences are from the direct experiences of metropolitan life, the more likely they are to construct imagined worlds" (35). For many in the global south, the imagined world of the north is one of big houses, fancy cars, leisure, and abundant wealth. This contrasts with the reality of poverty, disparity, and struggle which characterize the lives of many who live there.

The disjuncture between mediated messages of wealth and global inequality is intensified by the unique position of poor transnational migrants living and working within the U.S. "consumer republic." While they are at the bottom of the U.S. class hierarchy they often work in proximity to the wealthiest Americans, cleaning their homes and/or office buildings, bussing their dishes or preparing their food. They are exposed daily to the fancy clothes, cars, and gadgets that demarcate status in the urban upper class. Yet, although they witness the materialism and status games of the American elite first hand, few have the resources to participate. Many told me they would not be keen to join in even if they could. The aspirations of my U.S. respondents are modest, fitting with the traditional U.S. working class goals and ambitions.

In addition to the goal of family reunification, and the desire to own their own house, Honduran transnational migrants are focused on education for their children, family security, and well-being. Patricia, for example, told me that her goals for her children are, "that they study," and that "they be good people." She said that, "a lot of people think about leaving an inheritance for their children, a house, something they can live off of . . . Not me. I want them to study." Maria has similar ambitions for her children. "For my kid, I wish they all come out the right way, go to college, find good persons to marry. . . . You know your education is your life. Without an education, you go nowhere. So that's something that I always talk to my kids about, education." Some of my respondents equate education with future economic mobility. Martin Angel for example told me, "Well, for right now my aspiration is that my children get an education. I mean, I think that with an education they can make money, which is why I spend the money." He also has the goal of reuniting his family, and would like "to be with them anywhere." Paulo resonated with the aspiration of reunification, education and well-being. "Like all immigrants I want to get ahead. I want things to be better for my family, so that they don't lack things that they need. . . . I want my kids to be able to study, to go to university, and someday I want for us to be together in our own house."

The modest aspirations of transnational migrants residing in the United States are often complicated by the consumer ambitions and skewed perceptions of their families in Honduras. Although my research shows that most poor transnational migrants live modestly in the United States and in large part outside of the norms of consumer society, their families back home often desire, and in some cases demand, access to, and participation in American consumerism. Several of my respondents told me that they do not think their family back home understands how difficult life is in the United States, or how much they sacrifice in order to remit money and goods. Transnational families are not immune to the social and cultural impacts of the intensification of consumerism that has taken hold in the United States.

Juliet Schor (1998) found that consumer needs are constructed via emulation. Americans consume in relation to their reference groups, those who serve as basis for comparison. Schor argued that Americans have shifted away from the Veblenian era when they aspired to be like the social class immediately above (Veblen, 1899), to a new era of conspicuous consumption in which all social groups aspire to be like the elite. This shift, she learned, has been prompted by greater exposure to television, movies, and commercial advertising, which has dramatically increased American's perceived needs and aspirations for meeting them. Schor found that as inequality has

Transamerican Dreams

increased, neighborhood contact has decreased, and workplace contact for women has gone up. Media use has also increased at the same time that the there has been an upscaling of depictions of lifestyles on television. The confluence of these trends has resulted in a shift from horizontal to vertical emulation, or a change in reference groups.

Schor wrote,

> ... what we see on television inflates our sense of what's normal. The lifestyles depicted on television are far different from the average American's: with few exceptions, TV characters are upper-middle class, or even rich. . . . The more people watch television, the more they think American households have tennis courts, private planes, convertibles, car telephones, maids, and swimming pools . . . (80).

The impacts of this are two-fold. First, one's reference group is expanded to include television characters. Second, and an effect of the first, since those characters are more often than not living above the means of the social class they claim to represent, consumer needs are escalated based on false perceptions.

A similar phenomenon is happening transnationally. U.S. lifestyles and the lifestyles of the families who have high remittances are raising domestic aspirations in Honduras. Some respondents' reported that their family and kin networks imagine that in the United States everyone lives just like the people on television and that in America "everything is good."

Levitt (2001) termed the "ideas, behaviors, identities and social capital that flow from the host- to sending-country communities," *social remittances*. Images from the mass media, especially television, as well as the false messages of success that some migrants themselves transmit to friends and family, are social remittances which perpetuate the idea of the United States as a land of endless opportunity and riches. The transnational flow of the idea that in the United States everything is "good" or "easy," commonly results in family requests for more money and more consumer goods. This, in turn, puts pressure on transnational migrants in the United States to live up to what are often impossible expectations. When transnational migrants remit consumerist ideas, values, and culture to their families and communities, global culture is reproduced locally (Levitt, 2001). At the same time, perceptions of the United States may be distorted.

Doña Rosa, for example, told me that, "there are very advanced things there, very nice things. The evolution of the whole world is from the

United States, because it's a country of milk and honey, right? It's a blessing the United States. Because there isn't poverty, but rather everyone has a job, and lives well." Gloria shares Doña's Rosa's perception of America. She told me, "well, I've heard of the American dream, to go there to work to make . . . something for the future. . . . And there are a lot of material things. . . . What I really like is that the U.S. is super advanced. I see all the things that people have and all the people that study. Here in our country there's nothing. We're behind."

This imagery of life in the United States is further encouraged when transnational migrants visit Honduras wearing expensive clothes and jewelry, and boasting about the success they have found in the United States. Migrants who have little or no status in the United States can construct a new status in Honduras with little investment. By exploiting their transnational situation as poor laborers in the United States but showing off an image of wealth in Honduras where people do not know their U.S. reality, they can play the role of the elite. Many of my respondents told me that they visit Honduras with suitcases full of gifts and money. It is no surprise that their friends and family who have never been to the United States believe that they are rich, although they are poor by most any measure.

Luin Goldring (1998) found that because a migrant's local community knows his/her history and material reality before migration, acquiring and showing off material acquisitions in their local context is much more impressive than showing them off within their new U.S. community. Whereas David's new house means little to his co-workers in Chelsea, in his community in Honduras it has elevated him to hero status. Once the hero worship begins there is pressure for migrants to maintain the level of status they have projected. At the same time, by continuing to play the status game, they are willingly or unwillingly spreading the message that migration brings admiration as well as material rewards.

Levitt (2001) learned that remittances and transnational status games also affects the culture of home communities. Her research on transnational Dominican migrants shows that those who stayed in the Dominican Republic and lived off the remittances of their relatives became "addicted to a level of material comfort and consumption that they cannot sustain on their own" (86). She also discovered that the dependent standard of living that remittances create perpetuated a hunger for material goods and inspired a new measure of community status based not on values or ethics but on the amount and nature of consumer goods one has. When the Dominican migrants in Levitt's study returned to the Dominican Republic with no or few gifts they were considered "failures." Because migrants were fearful of failure, they commonly withheld their true stories of struggle and poverty from family members, and did all they could to present themselves as American successes.

Honduran transnational migrants reported being tormented by the skewed images their families have of life in America. Omar told me that his family's perception of life in the United States is completely false and as a result they expect him to send more money and more gifts than he can afford. When he tells them that he does not have the money, they simply do not believe him. It is so bad, he explained, that he now understands why some immigrants choose to cut ties to their family altogether. It is stressful, he told me, trying to live up to inflated expectations that are inspired by Hollywood and the role-plays of returning and visiting migrants.

> The truth is that all my family in Honduras believes that we are living well here, and that we are going to be millionaires. And we have been here four years, and it's a lie. The only good thing that has happened to me in this country is that I have learned a few words of English, and that my wife and I had another child. It's been brutal for us. We just work to live. We aren't able to save a penny. We haven't been able to do anything. . . . I have a nephew who has papers and he travels to Honduras every year. But I'm going to tell you that when he arrives there he is a liar. And when my mom asks him, 'How is my son's life in the United States?,' he tells her that I have a car. This is what happens. In Honduras only the people with money or credit have a car. All the Hondurans who return home tell lies. They wear the very best clothes that they have. And all of this influences the way Hondurans in Honduras imagine our lives in the States. They don't know that at times we don't even have the money to eat.

Dorotea echoed Omar's sentiments.

> Well, one thinks when they are in Honduras that things aren't so difficult in the United States. They think that everything is easy, that one gets work quickly that one can find one, two, or three jobs in the very first day, and earn a lot of money. They can't imagine all that you have to pay for here. It's because the people that go to Honduras to visit tell lies. They say that this is a country with a lot of good jobs. They are people who don't want their family and friends to know how difficult their life is here. So they go telling lies and ideas get formed in the other people's heads. When they lie and say that life is easy and there is a lot of work that pays a lot of money, others migrate here. The people who travel to Honduras only tell about the pretty things, they don't talk

about the difficulties . . . They want their families to think that they are having a lot of success. They want them to think that they work in nice offices, and they dress nicely every day. . . . The truth is that there are people here who take photographs in front of beautiful homes so that their families will think that they live there. Perhaps though they just were in front of the house because they work there cleaning it but they are to ashamed to tell them that.

Even young children perceive the United States to be a land of consumer dreams. Diego's son, who is five, does not remember his father well, but he frequently asks his dad for toys. Diego told me,

> My son in Honduras wants a motorcycle. He always tells me, 'You're a liar, you're a liar because you haven't bought me a motorcycle.' . . . He's only three, so it's not a real motorcycle. It's one of those that they use on the beach, but not one of the big ones, just a little one. He wants one of those . . . so I sent him a car that runs . . . a big one. I sent it to him for his birthday, and my dad sent him a bicycle. He has a bike, the car, other things, his bed, he has everything. . . . I sent him one of those remote controlled cars. He has everything, everything. Still he asks me, 'Why haven't you sent me the motorcycle?' 'Wait,' I tell him, 'I'm going to send it to you.'

When I visited Diego's house in Honduras, his son's eyes never looked up from the American cartoons he was watching on the big screen television the family had just bought with that month's surplus remittances.

There are some who have a more realistic view of immigrant life in the United States. Maira, for example, learned from her mother and her husband that life in America is not easy.

> When I go to Tegucigalpa and I look and think that that's what the United States must be like. Because everyone in Tegucigalpa is in a hurry, and I feel like the days go by like water. That's what I think. . . . And I don't believe it when people here say that everyone is a millionaire in America, because my mom has told me that for people who don't speak English life is really hard.

Lourdes said that she understands how difficult life is for her mom. Her mom has told her that it would not be good for her to come to the United States, because without an education you cannot find good work.

I know that sometimes when you go to the United States and especially when you go illegally, you suffer a lot. Sometimes my mom is hungry. She goes through a lot to help her family get ahead. I know that sometimes people are lucky, but in other cases they aren't. This makes me think a lot. Because I have many friends who tell me they have had luck. But my mom says she suffers a lot.

Families who communicate openly have the most realistic image of life in the United States. Yet, as Omar and Dorotea's experience demonstrates, transnational cultural flows perpetuated by other family and kin or by the media can overpower even the most truthful testimonies of sacrifice and struggle, putting added pressure on migrants to live up to the images of the enthusiastic American consumer by sending home more money and goods. In abiding by the consumer wishes and requests of family, the cycle of misperception is perpetuated.

CONCLUSION

The American dream has long been a cultural staple of the immigrant experience. For centuries, migrants have taken great risks and suffered emotionally through separation from their families. Honduran transnational migrants, like the Europeans who came before them, have hope and drive, and they employ many of the same strategies, working long hours and living frugally. But as my research shows, Honduran transnational migrants, like other migrants from the global south, are not finding the same success as Europeans. The opportunities for Hondurans in the United States are minimal at best. Still, as this chapter attests, Hondurans hold strongly to the belief that the American dream is within their reach.

Utilizing a transnational framework helps explain why the American dream remains a core element of the migrant imagination, even when most indicators show that a transnational migrant's possibility of attaining mobility are slim. Global inequality is such that Honduras' surplus labor pool has little outlet but migration for its survival. My respondents accept that "they did what they had to do" by coming to the United States to seek work and they believe that their sacrifice will make a difference in their families' lives.

Poverty is all most transnational migrants know. As such, even the smallest accomplishment that migration achieves can make a big difference in a family's daily life and in their perception of what is possible. Simple things by middle class American standards like a new washing machine, a television, a toy for a child, or a secure food budget, are celebrated as "successes" within the Honduran transnational community. Hondurans hold tightly to the American dream because in a transnational context it seems at least partially viable, and because they know little else than hard work and self-reliance. My respondents enjoy a sense of accomplishment because they have improved their lives and the lives of their families, no matter how modest the improvements have been.

They are also hopeful. My respondents are optimistic that someday their work will pay off and they will be able to be reunited with their families and to live comfortably and peacefully. This hope should not be underestimated. When one is far from her/his family, working in a low-wage job that is difficult at best and dangerous at worst, and when one gets no recognition from the host society for their strength and effort, hope is indeed a precious commodity. High levels of alcoholism and depression within the Honduran community are sad reminders, though, that not all can access this hope.

To understand the commitment transnational migrants have to the cultural ideology of the American dream and their complicated relationship to consumer society, a transnational analysis is required. Transnationalism is a means of enhancing family and community security by maintaining a resource base in two places. Similarly, transnationalism allows migrants and their families to construct their goals and strategies for fulfilling them outside of the confines of the nation-states in which they were born and in which they reside. The American dream becomes more viable when transmigrants transform it into a transamerican dream. Transnational migrants utilize the work and income-earning opportunities that the United States provides them to attempt the construction of their ideal life in Honduras. Of course there is a painful hitch to the story. Transnational migrants must be physically here and financially there to make it all possible; living for long periods away from family, kin, and their home country.

Conclusion
Para Seguir Adelante, To Continue Moving Forward

This research shows how deeply globalization is penetrating the daily lives of poor families. In Honduras, families increasingly use migration as a survival and mobility strategy because they cannot find work that pays a living wage. This has prompted a surge in transnational families. Consequently, children, parents, and caretaking kin are faced with the daily struggles implicit in long distance family maintenance.

I learned that the struggles of transnational families are economic as well as emotional. Economically, migrant remittances secure family survival and provide for material accumulation in Honduras. Yet, in the United States, transnational migrants work and live under difficult conditions, with little chance of moving up the economic ladder. Emotionally, family members on both sides of the transnational divide struggle with the effects of living in a permanent limbo. There are important theoretical and policy implications that emerge from these findings.

THEORETICAL IMPLICATIONS

This research challenges scholars to re-conceptualize family as a construction in which proximity is not implicit. Indeed, time and space cannot be taken for granted in the transnational lives of the families in this study. Thousands of miles and a heavily guarded border prevent parents from engaging in direct care and nurturance, and the politics and legal mandates of immigration make it impossible for most transnational families to know when or if their reunification will be possible. Transnational families represent a new family form, born out of the inequality of the global economy and reproduced by means of its dependence on a transnational division of family labor.

This transnational division of family labor is gendered. The productive labor of Honduran transnational families happens almost wholly in the north, with men spending more time in formal labor and remitting more of their earnings. Reproductive labor happens primarily in the south, and is done by women. While productive labor and the income support it brings to families tend to fall mostly along bloodlines, reproductive labor is a community endeavor. The central role of kin-networks in the maintenance of transnational families challenges conventional ideologies of the family which view children as the property of a nuclear family. As global inequality and poverty dictate, family survival is increasingly based on transnational community structures which are gendered at their core.

When Honduran families transnationalize, their lives become structured in large part by the transnational flow of dollars and goods between Honduras and the United States. Connected to the transnational flow of money and goods is a complex system in which meaning and culture are produced and transmitted. With every dollar sent, with every pair of blue jeans, compact disk, and television set, a message is transmitted about life in the United States. Whether intending to or not, transnational migrants who remit money and goods tell the story that they are living in a land of plenty. When the flow of dollars and goods is not accompanied by testimonies of what life is really like in the United States, including poor housing, long work hours, exploitation, cold, and loneliness, the mythological aspects of the American dream are perpetuated.

The exploration of transnational families that I have undertaken in this book presents a glimpse of the human side of transnational political, economic, and cultural forces. The lived experiences of transnational families speak to notions of survival, sacrifice, caretaking, and emotion. Migrant parents give up their cultural, national, and familial roots so that they can better provide economically for their children. My respondents testified to the prevalence of stress, abuse, and economic exploitation in their workplaces, as well as to the emotional burdens of loneliness and depression they carry with them in the United States. Yet they also claimed that these hardships were the only way "*para seguir adelante,* to move forward." Their daily struggles pose a challenge to scholars of migration, globalization, and family to bridge analyses of transnational life with policies which would better address the needs of families and support their drive to get ahead.

FAMILY REUNIFICATION IN THE FACE OF GLOBAL INEQUALITY

The research on transnational families tells a story about global inequality. Poverty and lack of opportunity in Honduras, and the concentration of capital in the United States, spur migration and thus, family separation. In

Para Seguir Adelante, *To Continue Moving Forward* 113

order to address the struggles of transnational families, we must first attend to the global mechanisms that make family well-being in Honduras so tenuous.

The families in this study have transnationalized because their needs were not being met in Honduras. Most did not have adequate work, housing, medical treatment, or educational opportunity. Meeting the needs of transnational families therefore entails investment in programs in Honduras to bolster the standard of living and economic opportunities. Genuine economic development is the ultimate answer to the problems facing transnational families.

At 5.4 billion dollars, Honduras has one of the highest per capita debts in the world (CIA World Fact Book, 2001). As such, Honduras has had to apply for high interest loans from the International Monetary Fund which have mandated the implementation of structural adjustment programs. The impact of structural adjustment programs on Honduras' health, education, and employment structures has been devastating. Designed to increase competitiveness and stimulate international investment, structural adjustment programs have been effective in building up Honduras' free trade zones, but ineffective in reducing poverty.

Ideally, the international community should forgive Honduras' debt and remove the mandates of structural adjustment to free up money for poverty alleviation programs, infrastructure improvement, and employment generation. In the mean time, cushioning the poor during adjustment by maintaining subsidies on food staples and protecting essential public services such as health, education, water, sanitation, and transport is crucial to the well-being of Honduran families. The poor, especially poor women, including the other-mothers in this study, would be better equipped to manage their households if their basic needs were guaranteed. Labor demand in the United States will exert less of a pull on poor families if life is more manageable in Honduras. Just economic policies would allow poor families the chance to stay together while attending directly to the reunification goals of those families who are already divided.

Until it is economically feasible for families to reunite in Honduras, families should be able to legally reunite in the United States. Currently, political and economic barriers prevent this from happening. Some families are kept apart because their member(s) working in the United States does not have legal residency. Those who do have residency often cannot afford to bring their families to the United States. In 1996 the commitment necessary to claim sponsorship for family members increased, making it even more difficult for poor immigrants to reunite with their families. In addition to these barriers, an application backlog has meant that even politically and economically qualified families frequently have to wait years to be legally reunited (Migration Information Source, 2003).

When legal reunification is not a possibility, families regularly opt to pursue illegal channels. Many wait until their children are old enough before they have them make the risky journey north. Years of separation followed by a dangerous and stressful attempt at reunification are common. If the U.S. government liberalized the requirements for family reunification this strain and uncertainty would be alleviated and the flow of undocumented migrants would be slowed.

Short of reunification, transnational migrants with Temporary Protected Status should be allowed to visit their families without restriction. Currently, migrants with Temporary Protected Status are not allowed to leave the United States unless they can prove that there has been a death or serious sickness in their family. Even when this is the case, my respondents tell me that the complicated paperwork, especially the requirement that they get signed permission from their employers, makes it a highly unfeasible option. Freedom of travel for those with Temporary Protected Status would strengthen families and enhance their emotional well-being.

Legalization

The most viable means of facilitating family reunification is through the legalization of all transnational migrants who are working in the United States. As my data reveal, permanent legal residency is essential to migrant mobility and enhanced family well-being. The respondents in this research who have legal residency have been able to secure employment that is both better paid and under better conditions than those who are undocumented. Legalization has also enhanced their emotional and material security, and it has allowed them the basic freedoms that native-born Americans take for granted. These include the freedom to travel, the right to fair housing, and better treatment in the work place, access to emergency public assistance, and the opportunity to participate in civil society. Legalization has also lent them a sense of dignity that continues to elude the undocumented.

Although September 11 put the legalization issue on the back burner for over a year, discussion on the issue has recently reemerged in Washington, and momentum is building at the grassroots. Fueling the effort is a growing acknowledgement that economic remittances are essential to maintaining economic and political stability in the global south. Also supporting this drive for legal amnesty is the realization that immigrant labor is a pillar of the U.S. economy.

Unionization

As I detail in chapter one, transnational migrants who are working in the United States face numerous barriers to their economic advancement. Historically, unionization has been the most viable route to securing worker's rights and supporting economic mobility among the working class. Whereas immigrants have previously been on the margins of the union movement, there has recently been a shift in union policy to embrace their struggle. In the spring of 2000, in a radical departure from their historical anti-immigrant stance, the American Federation of Labor-Congress of Industrial Organizations (AFL-CIO) declared their official support for an amnesty for all undocumented workers in the United States. With an estimated eight to twelve million undocumented workers in the United States based on analyses of the 2000 Census, the AFL-CIO came to realize that only by protecting the rights of those workers at the bottom of the labor pool could they effectively defend the wages and jobs of native-born Americans. I encourage all unions to follow suit.

Although my data show that many transnational migrants are hesitant to join unions, the success of the Justice for Janitors campaign in Boston, which worked with the Service Employees International Union (SEIU), demonstrates that this trend has the potential to change. Thousands of migrant workers, both documented and undocumented, joined the Justice for Janitors effort despite fears of losing their jobs or facing deportation. The terms of their victory included health coverage for one thousand part-time janitors, a wage increase of 30%, and paid sick leave for all janitors. Although the strike organizers did not achieve everything that they had hoped for, the majority of workers made some economic gains, which in turn boosted their families' security and well-being. Also, Boston janitors won respect from a public that had until then been virtually blind to their existence and contribution.

In many places around the country legalization and unionization campaigns are consolidating their efforts. This makes sense. Whereas legalization would help alleviate the fear that many undocumented workers have of joining union campaigns or supporting the creation of unions in their workplaces, unionization would insure that the potential economic benefits of legalization come to fruition. Unionization would attend to the practical economic needs of transnational migrants while asserting pressure on the basic structures of inequality in the global economy. The cross-fertilization of legalization and union strategies has the potential to achieve a more just existence for all transnational migrant workers and their families.

FUTURE STUDIES

There is great reason to be interested in and concerned about the future of poor transnational families. A generation of Honduran children is growing up without parents, and parents without their children. Grandmothers are raising two and sometimes even three generations of children. Families and communities have grown to depend on economic remittances for their livelihood. Transnational processes are redefining local and family culture and values. As the economic situation in Honduras worsens and the cross-border dependence of transnational families intensifies, these patterns will almost certainly continue. This reality challenges scholars of transnational migration to study the future ramifications of transnationalism for the daily lives of poor families.

I have focused little of this research on the second generation of transnational families. The children of transnational families, especially those who are raised in Honduras, merit further exploration. What will happen to those children who, with the support of remittances, attend secondary school or university in Honduras, but have little hope of finding work upon graduating? My data suggest that these children are assimilating into American culture by means of cultural and economic flows. Will their cultural assimilation partnered with little economic opportunity increase the push toward migration? If migration of the second generation does materialize when they reach adulthood, we may see a more educated undocumented labor force in the United States.

A related theme that emerges in these data is the growing pressure parents in the United States feel from their children in Honduras to channel surplus earnings and economic remittances into consumer purchases. Indeed, the intensification of consumerism and materialism, an issue that is gaining prominent attention among scholars in the United States, appears to be impacting the survival and mobility strategies of poor transnational families. Due to the limited financial resources of Honduran families, the stakes of this consumerism are high. Whereas there is a budding literature on the impact of consumerism on family well being in the United States (Schor, 1998; 2004), and on the identity formation and assimilation patterns of the transnational second generation in the United States (Levitt & Waters, 2002), there is little research that focuses on the consumer behavior, attitudes, and cultural assimilation of the transnational second generation that remains in its home country. And there is no research on how the consumer orientation of this second generation is affecting family well-being. There is a need for research that explores the relationship between the transnational second generation in Honduras and U.S. consumer culture and the impact of this relationship on family well being.

The gendered aspects of transnational families also demand more attention. How will transnational processes impact the gendered division of labor over in the long term? Research shows that women are increasingly migrating to work in the care industry in the United States (Ehrenreich and Hochshild, 2002; Hondagneu-Sotelo, 2001). As this takes hold in Honduras, who will take over the other-mother roles in poor families? Will we begin to see child shifting toward male caretakers?

In general, the data and analyses that I present in this book contribute a base from which to launch future studies that delve deeper into the ways in which global economic and cultural processes are restructuring family life. It is my hope that this book will open up opportunities for needed dialogue between scholars of family, immigration, poverty, and consumerism, and encourage a bridging of local and global analyses. And perhaps most importantly, it is my intent for this research to encourage more research "from below," bringing the people who most intimately experience the relationship between global inequality and everyday life to the forefront of transnational analyses. The words and experiences of transnational migrants should be fundamental to the construction of transnational migration theory and the policies which build upon it.

References

Alba, R. and V. Nee (1999). Rethinking assimilation theory for a new era of immigration. In C. Hirschman, P. Kasinitz, and J. DeWind (Eds) *The handbook of international migration: The American experience*. New York: Russell Sage.
Appadurai, A. (1996). *Modernity at large: Cultural dimensions of globalization*. Minneapolis, MN: University of Minnesota Press.
Aranda, E. (2003). Global care work and gendered constraints: The case of Puerto Rican transmigrants. *Gender and society*, 17, 609–626.
Aronowitz, S. (1998). *From the ashes of the old: America's labor and America's future*. Boston, MA: Houghton Mifflin.
Artico, C. (2003). *Latino families broken by immigration: The adolescents' perspectives*. New York: Lfb Scholarly.
Basch, L., Glick-Schiller, N. and C. Blanc (1994). *Nations unbound: Transnational projects, postcolonial predicaments and deterritorialized nation-states*. Canada: Gordon and Breach.
Bhabha, H. (1990). Introduction. In H. Bhaba (Ed.) *Nation and narration*. New York: Routledge.
Beneria, L. (1991). Structural adjustment, the labour market and the household. In G. Standing and V. Tokman (Eds.) *Towards social adjustment: Labour market issues in structural adjustment*. Geneva: International Labor Organization.
Bianchi, S. and J. Robinson (1998–1999). *Family interaction, social capital, and trends in time use*. Time diary data, University of Maryland.
Bluestone, B. and M. Stevenson (2000). *Greater Boston in transition: Race and ethnicity in a renaissance region*. New York: Russell Sage.
Borjas, G.(1999). *Heaven's door: Immigration and opportunity: Race, ethnicity, and employment in the United States*. New York: Russell Sage.
Brecher, J. (1997). *Strike!* Boston, MA: South End.
Breslin, J. (2002). *The Short Sweet Dream of Eduardo Gutierrez*. New York: Random House.
Bryceson, D. (2002). Europe's transnational families and migration: Past and present. In D. Bryceson and U. Vuorela (Eds.) *The transnational family: New European frontiers and global networks*. New York: Oxford.

Bryceson, D. and U. Vuorela (2002). Transnational families in the twenty-first century. In D. Bryceson and U. Vuorela (Eds.) *The transnational family: New European frontiers and global networks*. New York: Berg.

Burch, H. A. (1997). *Social welfare policy analysis and choices*. New York: Haworth.

Cancion, F. and S. Oliker (2000). *Caring and gender*. Thousand Oaks, CA: Pine Forge.

Chang, G. (2000). Disposable nannies: Women's work and the politics of Latina immigration. *Radical America, 26*, 5–20.

Chant, S. (1994). Women and poverty in urban Latin America: Mexican and Costa Rican experiences. *Poverty in the 1990s: The responses of urbanization*. UNESCO.

Charmaz, K. (2000). Grounded theory: Objectivist and constructivist methods. In N. Denzin and Y. Lincoln (Eds.) *Handbook of qualitative research*. Thousand Oaks, CA: Sage.

Chavez, L. (1998). *Shadowed lives: Undocumented immigrants in American society*. New York: Harcourt Brace.

Chiswick, B. (1978). The effects of Americanization on the earnings of foreign-born men. *Journal of political economy, 86*, 897–921.

Chomsky, N. (1985). *Turning the tide: U.S. intervention in Central America and the struggle for peace*. Boston, MA: South End.

Christians, G. (2000). Ethics and politics in qualitative research. In N. Denzin and Y. Lincoln (Eds.) *Handbook of qualitative research*. Thousand Oaks, CA: Sage.

CIA World Fact Book (2003). Washington D.C.: Central Intelligence Agency.

Cohen, Lizabeth (2003). *A consumers' republic: The politics of mass consumption in postwar America*. New York: Alfred A. Knopf.

Collins, P. H. (1992). Black women and motherhood. In B. Thorne and M. Yalom (Eds.) *Rethinking the family: Some basic feminist questions*. Boston, MA: Northeastern University Press.

"———." (1994). Shifting the center: Race, class, and feminist theorizing about motherhood. In E. Glenn, G. Chang, and L. Forcey (Eds.) *Mothering: Ideology, experience, and agency*. New York: Routledge.

Coutin, S. (2000). *Legalizing moves: Salvadoran immigrants' struggle for U.S. residency*. Ann Arbor, MI: University of Michigan Press.

Cranford. C. (1998). Gender and citizenship in the restructuring of janitorial work in Los Angeles. *Gender issues*, fall, 25–51.

Denzin, N. and Y. Lincoln (2000). Introduction: The discipline and practice of qualitative research. In N. Denzin and Y. Lincoln (Eds.) *Handbook of qualitative research*. Thousand Oaks, CA: Sage.

DeSipio, L. (2000). *Sending money home . . . for now: Remittances and immigrant adaptation in the United States*. A report of the Tomas Rivera Policy Institute, and the Inter-American Dialogue.

Dill, B. (1994). Fictive kin, paper sons, and compadrazgo: Women of color and the struggle for family survival. In M. Zinn and B. Dill (Eds.) *Women of color in U.S. society*. Philadelphia, PA: Temple University Press.

References

Dodson, L. (1998). *Don't call us out of name: The untold lives of women and girls in poor America.* Boston, MA: Beacon.

"———." and L. Schmalzbauer (Forthcoming). Poor mothers and habits of hiding: Participatory methods in family research. *Journal of marriage and family.*

Edin, K. and L. Lein (1996). *Making ends meet: How single mothers survive welfare and low-wage work.* New York: Russell Sage.

Ehrenreich, B. and A. Hochschild (2002). Introduction. In B. Ehrenreich and A. Hochschild (Eds.) *Global women: Nannies, maids, and sex workers in the new economy.* New York: Henry Holt.

Espiritu, Y. (1997). *Asian American women and men: Labor laws and love.* Thousand Oaks, CA: Sage.

Euraque, D. (1996). *Reinterpreting the "banana republic": Region and state in Honduras, 1870–1972.* Chapel Hill, NC: University of North Carolina Press.

Foner, N. (2000). *From Ellis Island to JFK: New York's two great waves of migration.* New Haven, CT: Yale University Press.

Foner, N. (1998). Benefits and burdens: Immigrant women and work in New York City. *Gender issues, 16,* 5–24.

Fouron, G. and N. Glick-Schiller (2002). The generation of identity: Redefining the second generation within a transnational social field. In P. Levitt and M. Waters (Eds.) *The changing face of home: The transnational lives of the second generation.* New York: Russell Sage.

Frank, R. (1999). *Luxury fever: Why money fails to satisfy in an era of excess.* New York: Free Press.

Garza, R. and B. Lowell (2002). *Sending money home: Hispanic remittances and community development.* New York: Rowman and Littlefield.

Glaser, B. and A. Strauss (1967). *The discovery of grounded theory: Strategies for qualitative research.* Chicago, IL: Aldine.

Glick Schiller, N. (1999). Transmigrants and nation-states: Something old and something new in the U.S. immigrant experience. In C. Hirshmann, P. Kasinitz, and J. DeWind (Eds.) *The handbook of international migration: The American experience.* New York: Russell Sage.

"———." and G. Fouron (1998). Transnational lives and national identities: The identity politics of Haitian immigrants. In M. P. Smith and L. Guarnizo (Eds.) *Transnationalism from below.* New Brunswick, NJ: Transaction.

"———.," L. Basch and C. Szanton Blanc (1992). Transnationalism: A new analytical framework for understanding migration. Basch, L., N. Glick-Schiller, and C. Szanton Blanc (Eds.) *Towards a transnational perspective on migration.* New York: New York Academy of Sciences.

Goldring, L. (1998). The power of status in transnational social fields. In M. Smith and L. Guarnizo (Eds.) *Transnationalism from below.* New Brunswick, NJ: Transaction.

Gordon, S. (1987). I go to tanties: The economic significance of child-shifting in Antigua, West Indies. *Journal of comparative family studies, 18,* 427–443.

Gramsuck, S. and P. Pessar (1991). *Between two islands: Dominican international migration.* Berkeley, CA: University of California Press.

Grosfoguel, R. (1999). 'Cultural racism' and colonial caribbean migrants in core zones of the capitalist world-economy. *Review, XXII, 4,* 263–87.
Guarnizo, L. and M. Smith (1998). The locations of transnationalism. In M. Smith and L. Eduardo (Eds.) *Transnationalism from below.* New Brunswick, NJ: Transaction.
Gupta, A. and J., Ferguson (1996). Beyond "culture": Space, identity, and the politics of difference. In A. Gupta and J. Ferguson (Eds.) *Culture, power, place: Explorations in critical anthropology.* Durham, NC: Duke University Press.
Harrison, B. and Bluestone, B. (1988). *The great u-turn: Corporate restructuring and the polarizing of America.* New York: Basic.
Heymann, J. (2000). *The widening gap: Why America's working families are in jeopardy and what can be done about it.* New York: Basic.
Hirsch, J. (2003). *A courtship after marriage: Sexuality and love in Mexican transnational families.* Berkeley, CA: University of California Press.
Ho, C. (1999). Caribbean transnationalism as a gendered process. *Latin American perspectives, 26,* 34–54.
Hobsbawm, E. J. (1975). *The age of capital 1848–1875.* London, U.K.: Weidenfeld and Nicholson.
Hochschild, A. (2002). Love and gold. In B. Ehrenreich and A. Hochschild (Eds.) *Global woman: Nannies, maids, and sex workers in the new economy.* New York: Henry Holt.
"———." (1997). *The time bind.* New York: Metropolitan.
"———." (1989). *The second shift: Working parents and the revolution at home.* New York: Viking.
Hochschild, J. (1995). *Facing up to the American dream: Race, class and the soul of the nation.* Princeton, NJ: Princeton University Press.
hooks, b. (1984). *Feminist theory from margin to center.* Boston, MA: South End.
Hondagneu-Sotelo, P. (2001). *Domestica: Immigrant workers cleaning and caring in the shadows of affluence.* Berkeley, CA: University of California Press.
"———." (1994). *Gendered transitions: Mexican experiences of immigration.* Berkeley, CA: University of California Press.
"———." and E. Avila (1997). I'm here, but I'm there: The meanings of Latina transnational motherhood. *Gender and society, 11,* 548–571.
Instituto Nacional de Estadistica—Honduras (2003).
Inter-American Development Bank (2001). *Remittances as a development tool.* Multilateral Investment Fund at the Inter-American Development Bank. Regional conference. Washington D.C. May 17th and 18th.
Kearney, M. (1995). The local and the global: The anthropology of globalization and transnationalism. *Annual review of anthropology, 24,* 547–565.
Keck, M. and K. Sikkink (1998). *Activists beyond borders: Advocacy networks in international politics.* Ithaca, NY: Cornell University Press.
Kibria, N. (1993). *Family tightrope: The changing lives of Vietnamese Americans.* Princeton, NJ: Princeton University Press.
Kim, M. (2000). Women paid low wages: Who they are and where they work. *Monthly labor review,* September, 26–29.

References

Krugman, P. (1997). *The age of diminished expectations: U.S. economic policy in the 1990s.* Cambridge, MA: MIT Press.

Latin American Bureau (1985). *Honduras: State for sale.* London, U.K.: Latin American Bureau.

Levitt, P. (2001). *The transnational villagers.* Berkeley, CA: University of California Press.

"———." and N. Glick Schiller (2004). Conceptualizing simultaneity: Theorizing society from a transnational social field Perspective. *International migration review,* 38, 1002–1039.

"———.," J. DeWind and S. Vertovec (2003). International perspectives on transnational migration: An introduction. *International migration review,* 37, 565–575.

"———.," and M. Waters (2002). Introduction. In P. Levitt and M. Waters (Eds.) *The changing face of home: The transnational lives of the second generation.* New York: Russell Sage.

Lincoln, Y. and E. Guba (2000). Paradigmatic controversies, contradictions and emerging confluences. In N. Denzin and Y. Lincoln (Eds.) *Handbook of qualitative research.* Thousand Oaks, CA: Sage.

Mahler, S. (1998). Theoretical and empirical contributions toward a research agenda for transnationalism. In M. Smith and L. Guarnizo (Eds.) *Transnationalism from below.* New Brunswick, NJ: Transaction.

"———." (1995). *American dreaming: Immigrant life on the margins.* Princeton, NJ: Princeton University Press.

Massey, D. (1999). Why does immigration occur? A theoretical synthesis. In C. Hirschman, P. Kasinitz, and J. DeWind (Eds.) *The handbook of international migration.* New York: Russell Sage.

"———." (1985) Ethnic residential segregation: A theoretical synthesis and empirical review. *Sociology and social research,* 69, 315–50.

"———." and M. Fischer (2000). How segregation concentrates poverty. *Ethnic and racial studies,* 23, 670–91.

Mead, L. (1992). *The nonworking poor in America: The new politics of poverty.* New York: Basic.

Mies, M. (1986). *Patriarchy and accumulation on a world scale.* London, U.K.: Zed.

Migration Information Source (2003). Washington D.C.: Migration Policy Institute.

Newman, K. (1999). *No shame in my game: The working poor in the inner-city.* New York: Knopf and Russell Sage.

"———." (1993). *Declining fortunes: The withering of the American dream.* New York: Basic.

Parreñas, R. (2005). *Children of global migration: Transnational families and gender woes.* Stanford, CA: Stanford University Press.

"———." (2001). *Servants of globalization: Women, migration, and domestic work.* Stanford, CA: Stanford University Press.

Pessar, P. (1999). The role of gender, households, and social networks in the migration process: A review and appraisal. In C. Hirschman, P. Kasinitz, and J. DeWind (Eds.) *The handbook of international migration.* New York: Russell Sage.

Pessar, P. and S. Mahler (2003). Transnational migration: Bringing gender in. *International migration review, 23,* 812–846.
Piore, M. (1979). *Birds of passage: Migrant labor and industrial societies.* Cambridge, U.K.: Cambridge University Press.
"———." (1975). Unemployment and the dual labor market. *The public interest, 38,* 67–79.
Piven, F. (2001). Globalization, American politics and welfare policy. *Annals of the American academy of political and social science,* 577.
Plaza, D. (2000). Transnational grannies: The changing family responsibilities of elderly African Caribbean-born women resident in Britain. *Social indicators research, 51,* 75–105.
Portes, A. and R. Rumbaut (1996). *Immigrant America: A portrait.* Berkeley, CA: University of California Press.
"———." and M. Zhou (1993). Gaining the upper hand: Economic mobility among immigrant and domestic minorities. *Ethnic and racial studies, 15,* 491–522.
"———." and R. Manning. (1986). The immigrant enclave: Theory and empirical examples. S. Olzak and J. Nagel (Eds.) *Competitive ethnic relations.* Florida: Academic Press.
Robinson, J. and G. Godbey, (1997). *Time for life: The surprising ways Americans use their time.* University Park, PA: The Pennsylvania State University.
Romero, M. (1992). *Maid in the USA.* New York: Routledge.
Sassen, S. (2002). Global cities and survival circuits. In B. Ehrenreich and A. Hochschild (Eds.) *Global woman: Nannies, maids, and sex workers in the new economy.* New York: Henry Holt.
"———." (1998). *Globalization and its discontents.* New York: The New Press.
"———." (1988). *The mobility of labor and capital: A study of international investment and labor flow.* Cambridge, U.K.: Cambridge University Press.
Schor, J. (2004). *Born to buy: The commercialized child and the new consumer culture.* New York: Scribner.
"———." (1998). *The overspent American: Upscaling, downshifting, and the new consumer.* New York: Basic.
"———." (1992). *The overworked American: The unexpected decline of leisure.* New York: Basic.
Schram, S. (2000). *After welfare: The culture of postindustrial social policy.* New York: New York University Press.
Sclove, R. (1997). Research by the people, for the people. *Futures, 29,* 541–549.
Scott, P. and J. Marshall (1991). *Cocaine politics: Drugs, armies, and the CIA in Central America.* Berkeley, CA: University of California Press.
Shaw, S. (1994). Mothering under slavery in the antebellum south. In E. Nakano Glenn, G. Chang, and L. Forcey (Eds.) *Mothering: Ideology, experience, and agency.* New York: Routledge.
Skocpol, T. (2000). *The missing middle: Working families and the future of American social policy.* New York: W. W. Norton.
Smith, R. (1998). Transnational localities: Community, technology, and the politics of membership within the context of Mexico and U.S. migration. In M. P.

References

Smith and L. Guarnizo (Eds.) *Transnationalism from below*. New Brunswick, NJ: Transaction.

"———." (1996). *The matrifocal family: Power, pluralism, and politics*. New York: Routledge.

Stack, C. (1974). *All our kin*. New York: Harper and Row.

"———." and L. Burton. (1994). Kinscripts: Reflections on family, generation, and culture. In E. Glenn, G. Chang, and L. Forcey (Eds.) *Mothering: Ideology, experience, and agency*. New York: Routledge.

Stewart, F. (1992). Can adjustment programs incorporate the interests of women? In H. Afshar and C. Dennis (Eds.) *Women and adjustment policies in the third world*. New York: St. Martin's.

Stoll, D. (1990). *Is Latin America turning protestant? The politics of evangelical growth*. Berkeley, CA: University of California Press.

Ueda, R. (1989). *Postwar immigrant America: A social history*. Boston, MA: St. Martin's.

United Nations Human Development Report (2003). *Millenium development goals: A compact among nations to end human poverty*. New York: United Nations.

United States Geological Survey (2003). http://mitchnts1.cr.usgs.gov/index.html

Veblen, T. (1899). *The theory of the leisure class*. New York: Macmillan.

Wallerstein, I. (1979). *The capitalist world economy*. Cambridge, U.K.: Cambridge University Press.

Waters, M. (1999). *Black identities: West Indian immigrant dreams and American realities*. Cambridge, MA: Harvard University Press.

White, M. and J. Glick (1999). The impact of immigration on residential segregation. In F. D. Bean and S. Bell-Rose (Eds.) *Immigration and opportunity: Race, ethnicity, and employment in the United States*. New York: Russell Sage.

Wilson, W. (1996). *When work disappears: The world of the new urban poor*. New York: Knopf.

Wyman, M. (1993). *Round-trip to America: The immigrants return to Europe, 1880-1930*. Ithaca, NY: Cornell University Press.

Index

A
Active member observation, 13
AFDC, 46–47
AFL-CIO, 115
African Americans, 22, 38–40, 53
Agrarian reform, 9
Alba, R., 4
Alcoholics Anonymous, 76, 87
American dream,
   Consumption, 3, 17, 102
   Global south, 22
   Inequality, 103
   Jobs with Justice, 20
   Migrants, 93, 106, 109–110
   Mythology, 112
   Transnational families, 18
Appadurai, A., 3, 7, 103
Aranda, E., 51–52
Aronowitz, S., 28
Artico, C., 53
Assimilation, 3–4, 116

B
Banana republic, 8, 10
Banco Atlantida, 9
Banco de Honduras, 9
Basch, L., 4–6
Beneria, L., 51
Bhaba, H., 5
Bianchi, S., 79
Bifurcated economy, 41, 23
Blood-mothers, 52
Bluestone, B., 22–23, 36, 38
Border crossings, 6
Borjas, G., 21, 37–38, 92

Brecher, J., 23, 28
Bryceson, D., 2–3, 6, 50, 54
Burch, H., 23

C
Campesinos, 26, 33
Capital, 3, 6, 23, 49, 112
Capitalism, 4–5, 51, 82
Capitalist, 18, 2, 35
Care networks, 17, 52, 55
Carework,
   Conceptualization, 77–78
   Emotional, 59
   Gender, 51, 55, 80–82, 84
   Honduras, 49, 82
   Theories, 51, 78
   Unpaid, 49, 78
Catholic church, 57, 86–87
Census, 12, 32, 39, 115
Chang, G., 30
Chant, S. 51
Charmaz, K., 13
Chase-Manhatten, 9
Chavez, L., 6, 25, 33, 52, 92
Child care, 72, 78–79, 82, 85
Child shifting, 53, 72, 117
Chiswick, B., 37
Chomsky, N., 10
Christians, G., 17
Civic participation, 12
Civil wars, 10, 51
Class,
   Colonial, 48
   Family, 2, 54
   Media presentations, 105

Migration, 7, 76–77
Mobility, 115
Polarization, 92
Privilege, 51
Race, gender, 21, 28, 77
Segregation, 39
Transnational, 7, 24
U.S., 23, 77, 79, 103–104, 109
Coffee, 9, 11
Cohen, E., 102–103
Collins, P. H., 44, 51–52
Colonial, 5, 9, 36, 47–48
Commercial agriculture, 25
Communication,
 E-mail, 66
 Honduras, 14, 78, 88
 Technology, 15, 50, 88
Community organizations, 87
Conspicuous consumption, 102, 104
Constructivist approach, 13
Consumerism,
 Globalization, 103
 Ideology, 7
 Media, 103–105
 Transnational context, 110
 Transnational families, 17–18, 62, 104–106, 116
 U.S. 93, 103–104, 109, 117
Contra War, 10
Counter-insurgency, 10
Coutin, S., 32–33
Cranford, C., 28, 30–31, 51
Culture of poverty, 23

D
Day care, 45, 47
Decolonization, 5
Deindustrialization, 5
Denzin, N., 12
Dependency, 8–9
Desipio, L., 60
Dill, B., 52
Dodson, L., 17, 43, 51–52
Domestics 30, 53
Dual labor market, 22

E
Edin, K., 23, 43, 51
Education,
 Inequality, 23, 35
 Social change, 12

Transnational migrant participation, 35, 38, 85–87
Worker, 29
Ehrenreich, B., 31, 117
El Salvador, 9–11, 20, 40
Entrepreneurial class, 12, 41
Espiritu, Y., 70
Ethnic enclaves, 41
Ethnic solidarity, 41–42
Euraque, D., 8–9
Evangelicals, 86–87
Export factories, 5
Export processing zones, 5

F
Family reunification, 71–72, 88, 104, 112, 114
Field research, 3, 12, 16
Foner, N., 28, 31, 50
Fouron, G., 3, 6
Frank, R., 103

G
Gangs, 39
Garza, R., 51, 60
Gender,
 Carework, 54, 72, 78–79, 81
 Economic incorporation, 30
 Education, 86
 Family division of labor, 51, 54, 89, 111, 117
 Inequality, 28
 Migration theory, 7–8
 Paid work, 52, 80, 84
 Race, class, 21, 77
 Survival strategies, 72, 112
 Time use, 14, 78–79
Glaser, B., 12
Glick-Schiller, N., 3–6, 50
Global north, 4, 52
Global south,
 Economic disruption, 5
 Family roots, 3, 5, 22
 Migrations from, 24, 28, 32
 Motherwork, 52
 Politics, 114
Goldring, L., 51, 99, 106
Gordon, S., 53
Gramsuck, S., 8
Grosfoguel, R., 21
Grounded theory, 11

Index

Guarnizo, L., 5–7
Guatemala, 9–10, 29, 40
Gupta, A., 5

H
Haiti, 10, 40
Harrison, B., 23
Hirsch, J., 6, 51
Ho, C., 51, 53
Hobsbawm, E. J., 5
Hochschild, A.
    Domestic service, 30
    Family carework, 40, 78–79
    "Second shift," 77–78
    Transnational mothers, 52
    Women migrants, 72
Hocschild, J., 92
Home ownership, 100–101, 103
Hondagneu-Sotelo, P., 8, 30, 52, 117
hooks, b., 54
Households,
    American, 105
    Costs, 42
    Fair, 114
    Housing, Conditions, 12, 39, 94, 112
    Kin-work, 52
    Migration, 8
    Poor, 113
    Power, 8
    Remittances, 60, 91
    Subsidies, 45, 47, 96
Human capital, 85–86
Hurricane Mitch, 11, 16, 51, 94

I
Identity, 4–5, 7, 89, 116
Illiteracy, 35, 66, 88
Immigrant rights, 19
Immigration policy, 87
Import substitution, 9
Inequality,
    Daily life, 90
    Global, 109, 111, 112, 115, 117
    Income, 38, 39
    Media, 103
    U.S., 23, 103–104
Informal economy, 11, 45, 51–52
International division of labor, 5
International Monetary Fund, 7, 113
Interpretive focus groups, 12, 17

J
Justice for Janitors, 26, 29, 115

K
Kearney, M., 3, 5
Keck, M., 7
Kibria, N., 8
Kim, M., 30
Kin-networks, 53, 55, 59, 105, 112
Kin-work, 52, 54, 58
Krugman, P., 23

L
Labor,
    Agricultural, 25
    Capital, Relation with, 5, 23
    Demand, 72, 113
    Division of, 30, 49, 51, 117
    Exploitation, 22, 106
    Globalization, 6
    Household, 78–79
    Informal, 52
    Issues, 87
    Low-wage, 22
    Mobility, 17, 49
    Non-wage, 53
    Participation, 16, 22
    Physical, 26, 27, 30
    Reproductive, 51, 89, 112
    Slave, 22
    Surplus, 20, 109
    U.S. economy, 114
Labor Force, 4, 22, 41
Labor Markets, 4, 22, 41
Labor unions, 23, 28, *also see* organized labor
Legalization, 35, 114–115
Leisure,
    Family, 33, 44–45, 114, 116
    Gender, 78, 84–85
    Involuntary, 84, 90
    Personal, 77
Levitt, P.,
    Remittances, 52, 106
    Social fields, 6
    Social remittances, 7, 105
    Transnational community, 3, 7
    Transnational family, 53, 99
    Transnational migration paths, 5
    Transnational second generation, 116
    Transnational theory, 4
    Transnational villages, 7

Lincoln, Y., 12–13
Literacy, 16, 66,
Living Wage Campaign, 13

M
Mahler, S.,
    Carework, 51
    Community solidarity, 45
    Gender and migration, 8
    Immigrant competition, 41, 44, 88, 94
    Immigrant ideology, 92–93
    Remittances, 39, 52
    Undocumented immigrants, 33, 39
    Human agency, 6, 38
Maquilas, 11, 16, 61, 91
Massey, D., 21, 23, 28, 38, 40
Mead, L., 21, 37, 92
Media, 29, 35, 103, 105, 109
Mediascapes, 103
Mies, M., 30
Minimum wage, 23–24, 31, 46, 62
Mobility,
    Barriers, 34, 37, 86, 94, 98
    Downward, 69
    Family, 33, 44–45, 114, 116
    Future, 104
    Income, 21
    Individual, 3, 42, 44, 47, 63
    Job, 21
    Opportunity, 23, 41, 47, 92–93
    Strategies, 2, 11, 21, 43, 111
    Upward, 3, 94, 97, 99
Model minorities, 42
Motherwork, 51–52, 54, 56, 64

N
Nationalism, 7
Neo-colonial, 8, *also see* Neo-liberal
Neo-liberal, 22, 37, *also see* Neo-colonial
Newman, K., 23–24
Nicaragua, 9–11
Nuclear family, 51, 54, 112

O
Observation 78, 83; *also see* Participant observation
Organized labor, 28, 43; *also see* Labor union
Other-mothers,
    Carework, 55–56, 67, 82, 117
    Community, 56–59

    Definition of, 52, 54
    Family maintenance, 53
Outsourcing, 52

P
Parreñas, R., 3–4, 8, 30, 52
Participant observation, 12–15
Personal Responsibility Act, 23
Pessar, P., 7– 8
Piore, M., 21–22, 24
Piven, F., 23, 28
Plaza, D., 53
Portes, A., 23, 38, 41, 92
Poverty,
    African American, 39
    Family, 36, 38, 49, 54, 107
    Global south, 4, 103
    Honduras, 8, 10–11, 48, 99
    Inequality, 38, 90, 112
    Marginalization, 47
    Methodological impact, 15
    Segregation, 39–41
    Structural roots, 39
    Undocumented migrants, 33
    U.S., 23, 32
    Wages, 92, 94, 99
    Workers, 20, 29
Proyecto Hondureño, 12–13

R
Reference groups, 104 105
Relativizing, 54
Remittances,
    Community, 7, 50, 60
    Daily life, 16, 61–62
    Dependence, 4, 116
    Economic stability, 114
    Education, 35, 46
    Family, 42, 50, 60, 63, 91
    Honduran economy, 11, 60
    Material accumulations, 108, 116
    Mobility, 21
    Motherwork, 64
    Obligations, 42
    Status, 106
    Survival, 21, 62, 111
Reproductive labor, 51, 89, 112
Revolution, 9, 54
Robinson, J., 78–80, 83–85
Romero, M., 30

Index

S
Sassen, S.,
  Deindustrialization, 5
  Global economy, 92
  Organized labor, 28
  Secondary sector, 21–22
  Service industry, 52
  Survival circuits, 72
  Transnational capital, 3, 7, 49
  Undocumented labor, 24
  U.S. economy, 23
Schor, J.,
  American dream, 103
  Consumption, 103–104
  Inequality, 83, 104
  Time use, 78–79
  Vertical emulation, 105
  Work/family, 43, 81–82
Schram, S., 23
Secondary sector,
  Carework, 36
  Dual-labor market, 22
  Latinos, 38
  Low-wages, 24
  Mobility, 33
  Poverty, 41
  U.S. economy, 32, 47, 83
Second shift, 77–78
Section Eight, 45, 47, 96
Segmented assimilation, 3
Segregation
  Class segregation, 39
  Occupational segregation, 39, 41, 93
  Racial segregation, 38–39
  Residential segregation, 39–41, 93
September 11, 13, 34, 98, 114
Service industry, 22–23, 30, 50, 52, 92;
Shaw, S., 53
Sikkink, K., 7
Simultaneity, 4
Skocpol, T., 23
Smith, R., 3, 5–7, 53
Social capital, 7, 105
Social change, 12
Social fields, 6
Social safety nets, 10
Stack, C. 44, 52–53
Standard Fruit Company, 8
Stewart, F., 51–52
Stoll, D., 86
Sub-contracting, 23

Survival circuits, 72
Survival strategies, 21, 50–51, 72, 78

T
Telenovelas, 2, 17, 85
Temporary agency, 25, 27, 75
Temporary Protected Status, 20, 25–27, 36
Temporary Protected Status restrictions, 114
Temporary work, 23, 25, 34, 83
Time diaries, 14, 18, 79–80, 82
Transamerican dream, 92–93, 100, 110
Transnational capital, 3
Transnational communication, 89
Transnational culture, 3, 109, 112
Transnational fathers, 54, 67, 69
Transnational labor, 3
Transnational mothers, 52, 68, 69
Transnational second generation, 35, 116–117
Transnational social fields, 6

U
Ueda, R., 50
Undocumented immigrants,
  Amnesty, 115, *also see* Legalization
  Census, 12, 32, 115
  Deportations, 13, 26, 30, 33, 35
  Education, 85, 116
  Financial contributions, 14
  Janitors, 19, 22, 115
  Legalization, 114, *also see* Amnesty
  Political power, 24, 39
  Poverty, 3
Unemployment, 10, 16
Unionization, 115
Unions, 115
  Vulnerability, 24, 28–29, 43, 65
  Wages, 76
United Fruit Company, 8

V
Veblen, T., 104
Violence, 10, 16, 29, 70, 86

W
Wallerstein, I., 5
Waters, M., 21, 116
Welfare reform, 23, 43, 71
White, M., 38
Wilson, W., 23, 39, 41
World Bank, 7
World Trade Organization, 7
Wyman, M., 7